asianvegetables

from long beans to lemongrass, a simple guide to asian produce | plus over 50 delicious, easy recipes

by Sara Deseran   photographs by Richard Jung

CHRONICLE BOOKS
SAN FRANCISCO

Library of Congress Cataloging-in-Publication Data:
Deseran, Sara.
    Asian Vegetables : from long beans to lemongrass,
a simple guide to Asian produce, plus over 50 delicious easy
recipes / by Sara Deseran ; photographs by Richard Jung.
        p. cm.
Includes bibliographical references and index.
ISBN 0-8118-2759-3 (pbk.)
Cookery (Vegetables) 2. Cookery, Asian. 3. Vegetables—Asia. I. Title.
TX801 .D48 2001
641.6'5—dc21   00-060350

Printed in China.

Food Styling: Pouké
Food Assistant: Samantha Campbell
Prop Styling: Carol Hacker/ Table Prop
Design: Ph.D
Chinese calligraphy: Jessica Yan

Distributed in Canada by Raincoast Books
9050 Shaughnessy Street
Vancouver, BC V6P 6E5

10 9 8 7 6 5 4 3 2 1

Chronicle Books LLC
85 Second Street
San Francisco, California 94105

www.chroniclebooks.com

to Mom, *of course*

acknowledgments

Thank you to my parents, both great cooks, who, despite never having eaten an Asian vegetable in their lives, jumped right in to offer their help. They hunted down one of the few Asian markets in Baton Rouge, Louisiana, dared to eat bitter melon, and, most important of all, schlepped groceries, tested and developed recipes, and researched my every query—all with endless enthusiasm. All my love to my husband, Colin, who sparked the inspiration for this book in the first place, consumed far more than his share of Chinese broccoli, continues to put up with my daily cravings, and keeps me on track. I could never have written this book without all three of them.

Like every book, this project was fully realized with the help of talented resources, including all of the accomplished contributors who graciously shared their recipes and advice. In particular, I'd like to thank Barbara Tropp, whose cookbooks I pored over long before I ever had the honor of meeting her; Kasma Loha-unchit, Richard Wong, and Sukhi Singh, who invited me into their homes and cooked up a storm; and Grace Young, a wonderful writer and now a good friend.

On the editorial end, thanks to Bill LeBlond, Stephanie Rosenbaum, and Amy Treadwell for believing in this book, plus Pamela Geismar and Leslie Jonath (a true genius). Sharon Silva—arguably the best copy editor in the West and certainly the most well traveled—humbles me with her eagle eye.

On the art end, thanks to Pouké and Samantha Campbell for making food without the froufrou, and to prop stylist Carol Hacker. Many, many thanks to Richard Jung for his devotion to this project. In a world buried in mediocre cookbooks, I am grateful to have been able to work with someone who shoots such beautiful photography.

Thanks to my recipe testers (i.e., talented friends) near and far who gave their time: To my parents, Katherine Cobbs, Beau Mixon and Melissa Stainback, Kate Horan, Sona Rao, Dave Clark, Jennifer Aaronson, Peggy Nauts, Ben Brand, and Lenna Lebovich.

I'd also like to acknowledge Tori Ritchie for giving me my start in food publishing, Deborah Kwan for being my own private 411, and last but certainly not least, Danielle, for always being there, ready to stir.

table of contents

foreword by Barbara Tropp

I came of gustatory age in the vegetable markets of old Taipei. I was a young poetry student at Taiwan University and a culinary cretin—a troglodyte among the Chinese, who seem genetically hardwired to enjoy good food. I had grown up in a neurotically hygienic American household, where orange cheese came presliced in individual wrappers, and peas were bought in a box or a can. At college in the '60s, I morphed into a fashionably emotional vegetarian, and lived mostly on spaghetti. (Hold the garlic, please.) Then life took a turn. Me of little appetite and no lust was plunked headlong into a world without solace: the traditional Chinese world of fresh vegetables. There they were, with their immense variety and hitherto unimaginable textures and tastes. I was terrified.

On my daily treks to the market, I must have been a great novelty: a Mandarin-spouting, scared, white girl surrounded by dirt. The market floors were dirt, pounded flat by the neighborhood denizens who came thrice daily to shop. The vegetables wore dirt, newly plucked from the earth. The merchants wore dirt, too—peasants, very vividly of the land, wearing soil in their creased faces, between their bare toes, and in the folds of their Chinese jackets. Vegetables were sold with stems, roots, shoots, and leaves. (Without shrink wrap, stickers, or bags.) There were mountains of them, in lanes a block long, heaped on tables or piled on the ground or balanced haphazardly on the wheels or seats of rickety bicycles.

This was a world without signs. There was nothing to inform a novice of what a fuzzy, green thing or a round, pink thing might be. Just piles of every imaginable color and shape, all of it startlingly fresh and alive. The farmers called out their wares with lusty voices and toothless smiles. I learned the vegetable names; I shopped every day. And I grew up, nudged by the gods to un-become a poetry scholar and slowly become a cook, and to trust dirt rather than fear it when it came to gifts from the land.

Sara's book is such a nudge, a happy trip down the aisles of America's newly integrated vegetable markets. She is a playful bunny in the field of Asian greens, and she will take away your fears. Now you can learn what to do with the lemongrass you find in the neighborhood supermarket, or (if you are lucky) how to identify that voluptuous, leafy green at your local farmers' market. You will learn that it isn't important what a vegetable is called (the name often changes even from village to village in Asia), but that freshness is key. You will learn that it isn't the puritanical middle of a vegetable that holds the flavor, but often the roots or the inner leaves, or some other part we Americans might carelessly ignore. Sara writes good recipes; they are inspiring as well as simple. So you will eat well.

This is a book of good substance and sustenance, too. You will march into the market and face Asian vegetables with new bravado. You will face the unknown and find it delicious.

introduction

ASIAN VEGETABLES IN AMERICA

In San Francisco, where I live, the sight of an elderly Cantonese woman half my size sorting through a box of lotus root, scanning for the tiniest bruise, is a familiar one. People pass me on their way home to cook dinner, their hands tightly grasping pink plastic bags spilling over with lush bundles of water spinach and spiky stems of lemongrass. I often exchange a smile with the man who runs one of my favorite markets as he slices off the stem ends of flowering Chinese broccoli, arranging them to face forward so that his customers can see their freshness. And, rather astonishingly, my local Safeway, in a very un-Asian part of town, now carries more than bean sprouts, snow peas, and bok choy. It has a relatively large section of Asian vegetables, stocking what used to be exclusively Chinatown items, from bottle gourd and Thai eggplant to fresh water chestnuts and even bitter melon, albeit slightly wrinkled. (I once asked the produce worker there, who happened to be Asian, if he had fresher water chestnuts stored in the back. He shook his head incredulously and said, "Go to Chinatown!")

Of course, these sights aren't unique to San Francisco. The U.S. Census Bureau predicts that by 2010 there will be 15.3 million Asians and Pacific Islanders living in the United States, so it's no

surprise that Asian markets abound in most metropolitan areas from New York to Los Angeles
to Chicago. And although there may not be large Asian communities in every town, my parents,
who live in Baton Rouge, Louisiana, can find everything from long beans to fuzzy melon at a
Vietnamese mom-and-pop store. In addition, the hottest American restaurants are dotting their
menus with soba noodles and fresh spring rolls, and chefs are incorporating Asian vegetables and
herbs into Western dishes. Echoing this trend, upscale catalogs like Shepherd's Garden Seeds are
hawking kaffir lime trees and rau ram.

THE THRILL OF THE MARKET

I became enamored with Asian cooking when I first moved to San Francisco in the early 1990s.
I was working in an office a few blocks from Chinatown (I still do), and my lunch breaks were
spent wandering up to the markets. I rarely bought anything—it was too unfamiliar—but I loved
to soak it all in: the musky smell of dried mushrooms and fish, the narrow aisles teetering with
strange condiments, the fish tanks alive with feisty tilapia.

What drew me the most was the flurry of activity at the produce stands. People swarmed around
piles of greens and gourds (elbows out, shoving accepted), smelling and scrutinizing. Here was
a confounding array of vegetables that I'd hardly ever seen before. That particular longing I
always get in a foreign country hit me—the desire to be let in. But here I was in my own country!
I wanted someone to lead me through the maze of vegetables, hold each one up, and tell me the
why's and how's. That was the beginning of this book.

A VEGETABLE IS WHAT A VEGETABLE DOES

The same elements of the Asian market that make it such a wondrous experience—the mounds
of unfamiliar produce, the inevitable bustle, the language difference—are also the things that can
make it intimidating. But if there's anything that I've learned about cooking with Asian vegetables,
it's that in the end, they're still just vegetables: plain and simple. You probably know more about
them than you think.

The most important rule of thumb is common sense. To an extent, a green is a green. If you're in a market staring in confusion at a bundle of *choy sum,* trust your judgment. If it looks a bit like spinach, it's probably going to taste like it—maybe a little more bitter, possibly more slippery. If you're weighing a taro root in your hand, just the fact that it's a tuber lets you know it will be starchy like a potato. When choosing for freshness, do as you would do with any vegetable: avoid bruises, soft spots, and mold; look for crisp leaves, vivid colors, and good smells. Remember, too, you're surrounded by experts. That woman next to you rummaging through a pile of lavender eggplants and victoriously pulling out the smallest and sleekest ones is unknowingly showing you the way. If you're feeling brave, ask her how she's going to prepare it. I've learned a lot by doing just that.

Once you've made your selection and you're ready to cook, be open-minded. It's likely that you'll be tasting some of these vegetables for the first time. Just like new music, you might have to try it twice to get it, three times to love it—and then you're hooked. I also encourage you to experiment. Although I've chosen recipes that are Asian in flavor, an Italian-style dish of Chinese mustard greens tossed with olive oil and Kalamata olives is delicious.

FRESH FLAVORS

With all fears set aside, cooking with Asian vegetables opens up a whole new world of textures, tastes, and traditions. When I first started researching this book, I went across the bay to take a tour of Oakland's ethnically diverse Friday morning farmers' market. It was led by Kasma Loha-unchit, a respected Thai cooking teacher and cookbook author. It struck me that every other vegetable Kasma held up was loved by Thais either for its bitterness or its texture—there's even a leafy green called slippery vegetable because it becomes mucilaginous when cooked—characteristics not generally favored by most Americans.

I figured I was missing out on something, so Kasma offered to make me a lunch of bitter melon, a gourd renowned for its astringent taste. She prepared it four ways: raw, dipped in a pungent fermented shrimp sauce; stewed with pork bones; in coconut curry; and stir-fried with egg. Bitter melon is an acquired taste, and on my own, I might have dismissed it. But Kasma pointed out how refreshing it is, showed me how to cook it with harmonious flavors, and explained its extraordinary medicinal value. With this information, I found that not only could I appreciate bitter melon, but that I quite liked it.

Similarly, I've become a proponent of stems. One day, I went shopping on San Francisco's Clement Street, sometimes called New Chinatown, with Barbara Tropp, a noted Chinese food authority. She pointed out a stack of greens and told me that the Chinese never discard the stems—they're just chopped up and tossed in first to allow more cooking time, and then the leaves follow. I've transferred this notion to other greens, from spinach to chard. Less waste, more texture—it makes a lot of sense.

TO YOUR HEALTH

Finally, you've been told to eat your vegetables, and with good reason. They are the cornerstone of a good diet. Cheap and readily available, they supply an abundance of vitamins, minerals, and fiber. Look at the traditional Asian diet and you will see that vegetables are flavored with a bit of meat—not the other way around, as is the American way.

The United States Recommended Dietary Allowance is three to five servings of vegetables a day (and this is minimal). But even with the best intentions, most of us find it hard to slide in more than a salad here or a side of green beans there. I often find myself at the supermarket, staring blankly at yet another perfectly misted, oddly proportional lineup of the same old vegetables—broccoli, carrots, lettuce, the odd pink tomato—and I shrink back, uninspired to cook anything. Not only do Asian markets offer a whole new group of possibilities to add to your repertoire, but the excitement of shopping at them is infectious. I hope that, with the help of this book, the Asian market will draw you in, too, and that suddenly you'll be nudging someone over to get at the perfect luffa squash, sniffing out a bundle of Thai basil, and finding it all a thrill.

using this book

WHAT'S IN A NAME?

Some Asian vegetables have not been assimilated into Western culture, and therefore lack English names. But what makes matters more confusing is that every country—and sometimes regions within countries—has its own name for each vegetable, and English translations can vary wildly. Chinese broccoli, for instance, is also called Chinese kale, but like many of the vegetables, you'll often hear it called by its Cantonese name, which may be spelled either *gai lan* or *gai larn*. And then, of course, there's a host of other names for Chinese broccoli, depending on to whom you're talking, that is, whether the person be Thai or Vietnamese or Cambodian.

This can be frustrating, but if you can recognize the vegetables at the market, for the most part, it doesn't matter what they're called. That's why this book has clear color photographs to make identifying them easy. I have listed each vegetable under the name you are most likely to encounter, followed by other English and foreign names when appropriate. To help you further, I've divided the book by type of vegetable rather than name: leafy greens; roots, shoots, and bulbs; squashes and gourds; beans and things (which includes everything from eggplant to mushrooms); and herbs and aromatics.

VEGETABLES 101

This book is meant to be an Asian-vegetable primer, not an all-encompassing encyclopedia. My apologies for the vegetables I've neglected, from chrysanthemum leaves to arrowhead, kudzu to kohlrabi. A complete list of Asian vegetables would be nearly endless! Instead, I've selected vegetables that you'll find in most well-stocked American supermarkets, along with ones that I believe will be coming to you soon. Some vegetables, such as lotus root, are unique to Asian markets but well worth searching out. And although fresh turmeric isn't very common, I enjoy cooking with it, so I wanted to show you how it's done.

Most of the items that follow are found readily at Chinese markets, but some, like the herbs and certain chilies, are typically Southeast Asian, or, like *mizuna*, are commonly Japanese. And remember, if you can't find something in your local market, don't hesitate to ask. With enough demand, your grocer just might start carrying it.

leafy and green

The most confusing terrain of the Asian vegetable world is the endless array of greens, few of which have standard names. Although I haven't divided them as such, many of the entries, including bok choy, Chinese broccoli, *choy sum*, napa cabbage, *mizuna*, mustard cabbage, and *tatsoi*, are part of the big cabbage clan. For the most part, these are available year-round, but like any hearty greens, they are best when there is a bit of a nip in the air.

My best advice is to learn to recognize Asian greens by sight. And since many of them are interchangeable, if you go home with the wrong bunch, just cook it, enjoy it, and chalk it up to experience—a healthy one. When you return to the market next time, you'll be that much more knowledgeable. There's little waste in Asian cooking, so unless I specify otherwise, you can assume that the entire green is eaten, stems and all. In general, when selecting greens, look for perky leaves that have deep color and moist, crisp stems.

leafy and green

amaranth

ALSO KNOWN AS: *Chinese spinach,* yin choy *(Cantonese)*

Two kinds of amaranth are found in the market: red and green. Both have a mild taste that recalls spinach. Except for color, they look similar, but the red variety, with its green leaves, the veins stained a beet red, is easiest to spot and can be so striking that it's hard to decide whether to cook it or use it as a centerpiece. Amaranth is by no means unique to Asian cuisine. It's cultivated all over the world. Although it has yet to hit mainstream America, its popularity has increased, and I've spied it at farmers' markets and gourmet grocery stores, as well as Asian markets. It is sold in different stages: in bundles of young stems with delicate leaves that beg to be used that minute, and more mature, when the wide, oval leaves that come to a point are a bit crinkly and have a sharper flavor.

amaranth

SELECTING AND STORING: Choose bunches with good color and a just-harvested look. Store in a loosely closed plastic bag in the refrigerator crisper. Depending on its maturity, amaranth should be used immediately or within the next couple of days.

HOW TO USE: Older or tough parts of the stems should be removed; otherwise, the entire plant is edible. Rinse well to rid the leaves of any sand. Amaranth is stir-fried, cooked in soups, steamed, and, in its youngest, most tender form, eaten raw in a salad. Although it can replace spinach in any recipe, amaranth will cook a little faster.

noodle soup with roast duck and amaranth

I love the crisp, sweet-salty roast ducks that hang in the windows of delicatessens in every Chinatown. Paired with greens like amaranth, Chinese broccoli, choy sum, or even spinach, these glistening birds are the perfect answer to an easy meal. Don't be shy about stepping inside and placing an order. Duck is sold either half or whole, chopped into pieces, bone and skin intact. As an alternative, you can use a good roast chicken, and use a cleaver or heavy knife to cut it in half, then into 1-inch-thick pieces. The process of using chopsticks to eat pieces of duck on the bone—delicately—requires a finesse that I have yet to master (but I kind of relish the bit of mess).

SERVES 4 *If you have squeamish eaters, you can always bone the meat before adding it to the soup.*

2 tablespoons canola oil

¼ cup finely chopped shallot

5 ½ cups chicken broth

1½-inch piece fresh ginger, bruised

2 star anise

½ cinnamon stick

¾ pound fresh Chinese egg noodles

1 tablespoon fish sauce

Kosher salt to taste

½ pound amaranth, tough stem ends discarded and cut into 4-inch pieces

½ Chinese roast duck, about ¾ pound, cut into thick pieces (see recipe introduction)

In a large pot over medium-high heat, heat the oil. Add the shallot and sauté for about 15 seconds until fragrant. Add the broth, bring to a simmer, and reduce the heat to low. Add the ginger, star anise, and cinnamon stick, then cover, and simmer for 30 minutes to infuse the broth with the spices.

Meanwhile, bring a large pot filled with water to a boil. Add the noodles and allow to cook for 2 to 3 minutes, or until tender. Drain and set aside.

Add the fish sauce and salt to the broth and remove and discard the ginger, cinnamon stick, and star anise. Add the amaranth and allow to cook down for about 1 minute. Add the duck pieces and allow to simmer for 1 minute more, to heat through.

Divide the noodles among 4 bowls, and ladle the soup over them, dividing the pieces of duck evenly. Serve at once. Put out a bowl for diners to use for their discarded bones.

bok choy

ALSO KNOWN AS: *Chinese white cabbage,* pak choy *(Cantonese)*

Bok choy has become the model Asian vegetable. Its crisp, succulent stems and mild-tasting leaves have been the darling of fusion chefs and an easy sell to the Western palate. Cultivated in China since the fifth century, this venerable green is now stocked by most mainstream grocery stores. A number of kinds of bok choy are sold in markets here. The one known popularly as simply bok choy, its Cantonese name (also sometimes spelled *pak choy*), is the size of Swiss chard, with dark green, crinkly leaves and broad, smooth white stems. *Bok choy sum* is almost identical but with the yellow flowers of *choy sum* (page 24). It is sold in both baby and adult forms. My personal favorite is Shanghai bok choy, with distinctive pale green, spoonlike stems. It's almost always sold in its infant stage and is what most Western markets carry and label "baby bok choy."

bok choy (baby bok choy, "bok choy," bok choy sum)

SELECTING AND STORING: In many Asian markets, baby versions of Shanghai bok choy and *bok choy sum* are sold by the dozen, prepackaged in a plastic bag. Large bok choy is rather resilient and can be stored in a loosely closed plastic bag in the refrigerator crisper for up to 4 days. Baby bok choy of any variety can yellow more quickly and should be used as soon as possible.

HOW TO USE: To use the large variety, slice the stems crosswise and add them to a stir-fry or soup before you toss in the leaves, to give the stems a little extra time to cook. When very small, baby bok choy can be cooked whole. If large, halve lengthwise. Bok choy is versatile and is used in everything from stir-fries to braised dishes. The hearts are served as a delicacy.

braised short ribs with hearts of bok choy

As refreshing and light as bok choy can be in a stir-fry, it also lends itself well to slow cooking, as in this winter stew. I like to use the hearts of baby bok choy, just throwing them in at the very end. Instead of cooking this dish on the stove top, I've done it in the oven, which results in less of a mess. Serve a crusty baguette alongside in place of rice. The broth is so good that everyone will want to sop up the last drop.

SERVES 4

8 beef short ribs (about 4 pounds total)

2 teaspoons kosher salt

1 large yellow onion, halved and thinly sliced

1 tablespoon finely chopped garlic

1 tablespoon finely chopped fresh ginger

¼ cup soy sauce

3 tablespoons ketchup

2 tablespoons rice vinegar

1 teaspoon freshly ground pepper

1 teaspoon Korean red pepper flakes

1 tablespoon sesame seeds

1½ cups water

2 carrots, peeled and sliced ½ inch thick (about 1 cup)

4 heads baby bok choy, about 1 pound, bottoms
   trimmed, leafy tops removed, and hearts
   quartered lengthwise

Preheat the oven to 450°F. Place the ribs in a Dutch oven or other large ovenproof pot with a lid and sprinkle with the salt. Top with the onion slices. Cover and roast for 30 minutes.

In a bowl, mix together the garlic, ginger, soy sauce, ketchup, rice vinegar, ground pepper, red pepper flakes, and sesame seeds. Remove the pot from the oven and pour the sauce over the ribs. Add the water, and stir to mix. Turn the oven down to 350°F, re-cover the pot, and continue to cook for up to 2 hours longer, or until the beef is fork tender.

Add the carrots and baby bok choy, cover, and cook, turning the vegetables occasionally if necessary to let them cook evenly, for 10 to 15 minutes, or until the carrots are tender and the bok choy is more tender than crisp.

To serve, using tongs, transfer the braised ribs and the vegetables to a shallow serving bowl and ladle the hot broth over them.

bok choy, water chestnut, and bacon chow mein

SERVES 4

You might not think of bacon as Chinese, but salt curing is an ancient tradition in China, and slabs of cured pork belly are a common sight in Asian butcher shops. The slabs are often cubed and used to flavor stir-fries, soups, and clay pots. In this hearty dish, American bacon, fresh water chestnuts, bok choy, and sugar snap peas are all tossed together with a generous tangle of thick, chewy noodles. For a special presentation, halve the snap peas lengthwise, exposing the little peas inside.

1 pound fresh thick Chinese noodles, preferably Shanghai or chow mein style

1 teaspoon plus 1 tablespoon sesame oil

3 tablespoons oyster sauce

1 tablespoon soy sauce

2 tablespoons rice vinegar

1 teaspoon sugar

½ cup chicken broth

1 tablespoon canola oil

4 slices bacon, cut into 1-inch pieces

1-inch piece fresh ginger, peeled and slivered

2 small heads baby bok choy, bottoms trimmed, separated into leaves, and each leaf halved lengthwise

½ cup sugar snap peas, trimmed and halved lengthwise

5 fresh water chestnuts, peeled and sliced into coins

1 tablespoon cornstarch dissolved in 2 tablespoons water

Bring a large pot filled with water to a boil. Add the noodles, separating them as you go to keep them from sticking to one another. Cook for 3 to 5 minutes, or until tender. Drain the noodles and place in a large bowl. Toss with 1 teaspoon sesame oil. Set aside.

In a small bowl, combine the 1 tablespoon sesame oil, oyster sauce, soy sauce, rice vinegar, sugar, and chicken broth; set near the stove. In a wok or large, deep skillet over medium-low heat, heat the canola oil. Fry the bacon for 1 to 2 minutes, or until it is just beginning to crisp. Add the ginger and continue to cook for 15 seconds. Turn the heat to high, add the bok choy, snap peas, and water chestnuts, and stir-fry for about 1 minute, or until the bok choy leaves begin to wilt. Add the oyster sauce mixture, bring to a simmer, stir in the cornstarch mixture, and cook for about 15 seconds, or until the sauce thickens a bit. Add the noodles and toss as you would a salad, using a spatula or fork in each hand. Cook for 1 minute more to heat the noodles. Serve at once.

chinese broccoli

芥
蘭

ALSO KNOWN AS: *Chinese kale,* gai lan *(Cantonese)*

Except for its stout stems and slate green color, this vegetable, which many markets sell under its Cantonese name, *gai lan,* has little resemblance to the broccoli we know. Like *choy sum* (page 24) and *bok choy sum* (page 17), it is always sold flowering, although in this case the flowers are white instead of yellow (and just to throw you off track, it's often sold when the buds are still closed). The leaves are dark green, round, and fanlike, and can be slightly waxy in appearance. Although they're consumed as well, the sweet, asparagus-flavored stems are what you are seeking.

chinese broccoli

SELECTING AND STORING: Chinese broccoli is usually displayed stacked with the stems facing out. Look for the slimmest stems you can find, without any white holes visible on the cut ends. Store the greens in a loosely closed plastic bag in the refrigerator crisper for up to 5 days.

HOW TO USE: Trim off the tough stem ends. If the stems are extra thick, use a vegetable peeler to remove the skin, and then halve the stems lengthwise before cooking. In restaurants, Chinese broccoli is often served drizzled with oyster sauce, and it also holds up well to a good and garlicky stir-fry with beef. It should be served crisp-tender. *Choy sum* is a good substitute.

chinese broccoli with oyster sauce

SERVES 4
as a side dish

The Chinese broccoli in this dish is interchangeable with just about any other green, from choy sum to bok choy. Serve it over noodles or with rice, and you've put dinner on the table in about ten minutes. Although Chinese broccoli is not as delicate as some greens and won't absorb oil as quickly, if you have only a small wok or skillet, it is best to cook it in two batches.

2 tablespoons Shaoxing wine

1 tablespoon soy sauce

2 tablespoons oyster sauce

1/4 teaspoon sugar

1/2 teaspoon kosher salt

1/4 cup chicken broth or water

2 tablespoons canola oil

1 tablespoon finely chopped garlic

1 teaspoon finely chopped fresh ginger

3/4 pound Chinese broccoli, tough stem ends discarded and stems and leaves cut into 3-inch pieces

2 teaspoons cornstarch dissolved in 4 teaspoons water

In a small bowl, combine the Shaoxing wine, soy sauce, oyster sauce, sugar, salt, and chicken broth or water.

In a wok or large, deep skillet over medium-high heat, heat the oil. Add the garlic and ginger and stir-fry for 15 seconds until fragrant. Add the Chinese broccoli, toss well, and add the oyster sauce mixture. Cover and let the Chinese broccoli cook for another 3 to 5 minutes, or until crisp-tender. Add the cornstarch mixture, toss to combine, and cook for about 30 seconds, or until the sauce thickens a bit. Transfer to a platter or bowl and serve at once.

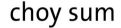

choy sum

ALSO KNOWN AS: *Chinese flowering cabbage, oil vegetable,* yow choy *(Cantonese),* yow choy sum *(Cantonese)*

If the name for any Asian vegetable is hard to pin down, it's the one for this pretty flowering green, distinctive because of the little vivid yellow flowers that blossom between its broad, oval green leaves. I call it *choy sum,* but you'll hear it called *yow choy* just as often. Related to rape, this vegetable is also used for its oil. Not to be confused with *bok choy sum* (page 17), the stems are pale green and no bigger than your pinkie. Slightly mustardy in flavor, it's versatile and one of the most popular vegetables in China.

choy sum

SELECTING AND STORING: *Choy sum* is often arranged in stacks with the stems facing out, so that you can quickly survey which bunch is the freshest by avoiding any with white holes at the base. Make sure the flowers are not bolting. Look for tight buds that are just beginning to blossom. *Choy sum* can be stored in a loosely closed plastic bag in the refrigerator crisper for up to 4 days.

HOW TO USE: With the exception of a slightly shorter cooking time (because of the thinner stems), *choy sum* is for the most part interchangeable with Chinese broccoli. Chard makes a good substitute as well. It's most often steamed, used in stir-fries, and thrown into soups at the last minute and should be served crisp-tender. I like to toss the uncooked yellow flowers in green salads.

steamed shrimp-and-greens dumplings

SERVES 6
as an appetizer

The dumpling filling can be made several hours ahead of time, although it's best to fold the dumplings right before you are ready to steam them. Use the thinnest wrappers you can find. I like the round ones labeled sue gow *made by New Hong Kong Noodle Company in San Francisco, but you can buy Japanese* gyoza *wrappers, too. Makes about 40 dumplings.*

FILLING:

¾ pound *choy sum*, stems removed and reserved
   for another use

½ pound shrimp, peeled, deveined, and finely
   chopped

¼ pound ground pork

¼ cup chopped green garlic chives

2 teaspoons finely chopped fresh ginger

3 fresh water chestnuts, peeled and finely chopped
   (about ⅓ cup)

1 tablespoon soy sauce

1 teaspoon Shaoxing wine

1 teaspoon sesame oil

¼ teaspoon sugar

1 egg white

About 40 round wrappers (see recipe introduction)

DIPPING SAUCE:

½ cup soy sauce

½ cup distilled white vinegar

1 tablespoon sesame oil

1 green onion, green part only, thinly sliced

To make the filling, bring a large pot filled with water to a boil. Add the *choy sum* and parboil for about 3 minutes. Drain, rinse under cold water, and squeeze out any excess liquid. Chop finely.

In a bowl, combine the chopped greens with all of the remaining filling ingredients.

To make the dumplings, fill a small bowl with water and keep it by your side. Lay a wrapper on a dry surface, dip your finger into the bowl of water, and use it to dampen the outer edges of the wrapper. Spoon a heaping teaspoon of the filling onto the center. Fold the wrapper over the filling in half and seal it, pushing out any air bubbles. Set aside on a paper towel or a piece of parchment paper and cover with a clean, dry towel. Continue in this manner to make the rest of the dumplings.

Prepare a bamboo steamer or a metal steamer rack by brushing it with oil. Place the dumplings inside; do not allow them to touch or they will stick to one another. Fill a wok or large pot half-full with water, bring to a gentle boil, and position the steamer above the water. Cover and steam for 5 to 7 minutes, or until the filling is cooked through. Meanwhile, in a small bowl, combine all the ingredients for the dipping sauce and mix well.

Remove the dumplings to a plate or serve them straight from the bamboo steamer. Steam and serve the remaining dumplings in the same way.

jap chae

When I go out for Korean food, I always order jap chae, *a comforting dish of glassy sweet potato noodles stir-fried with beef and vegetables. If you can't find sweet potato noodles (available in Korean markets), cellophane noodles will work as a substitute, but they lack the chewy texture and thickness. Recipes for* jap chae *often call for spinach, but here I use* choy sum, *which has more substance. Although you can matchstick-cut the carrot by hand, a Japanese mandoline eases the task and produces precise results. To get the beef ultrathin, try freezing it partially before cutting on an angle with a very sharp knife.*

SERVES 4

½ pound flank steak, thinly sliced into 2-inch-long pieces

1 teaspoon kosher salt

2 ½ teaspoons brown sugar

3 teaspoons finely chopped garlic

½ pound *choy sum*, tough ends discarded and stems and leaves cut into 2-inch pieces

¼ cup soy sauce

1 ½ teaspoons sesame oil

2 tablespoons canola oil

1 carrot, peeled and cut into 2-inch matchsticks

1 small red bell pepper, seeded and cut into 2-inch matchsticks

½ yellow onion, quartered and thinly sliced crosswise

½ pound dried sweet potato noodles or cellophane noodles, soaked in hot water to cover for 20 minutes and drained

In a bowl, toss the beef with the salt, ½ teaspoon of the brown sugar, and 1 teaspoon of the garlic, and let marinate for at least 15 minutes or for up to 1 hour.

Meanwhile, bring a large pot filled with water to a boil. Add the *choy sum* and parboil for 2 minutes, or until just wilted. Drain, rinse under cold water, squeeze out any excess liquid, and set aside.

In a small bowl, stir together the remaining 2 teaspoons each garlic and brown sugar, the soy sauce, and the sesame oil. Set aside.

In a wok or a large, deep skillet over high heat, heat 1 tablespoon of the canola oil. Swirl to coat the pan and add the beef. Let it sit undisturbed for about 1 minute. Turn the beef over and sear for another 1 minute. Using a slotted spoon, transfer to a plate and set aside. Pour off any fat from the pan, then wipe it out with a paper towel.

Add the remaining 1 tablespoon canola oil to the pan over high heat. Once it's hot, add the carrot, the bell pepper, and onion and stir-fry for 1 minute. Add the *choy sum* and the noodles, and pour in the sauce. Add the beef. Using a spatula or fork in each hand, toss the noodles with the vegetables until well combined. Let the noodles cook for another 2 minutes, or until soft but chewy. Serve immediately.

水
菜

mizuna

This lovely green stars in nearly every baby salad mix. Easy to pinpoint for its feathery leaves, you'll find it sold separately (although usually still in its infant stage) at some gourmet stores and farmers' markets. If you're searching for mature *mizuna,* don't look in Chinatown. Instead, head to a Japanese grocery where it is sold as it grows, in a clump, much like frisée. Or try growing *mizuna* yourself. I did, and now, years later, it's still popping up around my yard like a weed.

mizuna

SELECTING AND STORING: Look for leaves that are deep green. Store *mizuna* in a loosely closed plastic bag in the refrigerator crisper for up to 4 days. Younger leaves may wilt more quickly.

HOW TO USE: Although the leaves can be eaten raw tossed with a good vinegary dressing, I find that, like spinach, the slightly bitter and glossy character of young *mizuna* makes it a perfect candidate for wilted salads. Take a lead from chefs and tuck baby *mizuna* under a fillet of fish or mix it with other little greens. The mature vegetable is used like nearly every Asian green, stir-fried, steamed, and in soups.

wilted mizuna and grilled steak salad

SERVES 4

I like to use mizuna for this recipe because its slightly spicy flavor holds up to the hearty slices of steak, and it doesn't lose its character when it wilts. Baby mixed greens can be substituted, but I'd suggest barely warming the dressing so as not to devastate the more tender greens.

MARINADE:

1½ teaspoons kosher salt

1 teaspoon freshly ground pepper

1 tablespoon finely chopped garlic

1 tablespoon finely chopped fresh ginger

1 tablespoon tamari or soy sauce

1½ teaspoons brown sugar

1 pound tri-tip or sirloin tip steak

1 red onion, sliced crosswise in ½-inch-thick rounds

1 teaspoon canola oil

½ teaspoon kosher salt

MISO DRESSING:

¼ cup water

2 tablespoons red miso

1 tablespoon mirin

2 tablespoons distilled white vinegar

1 teaspoon tamari or soy sauce

1 teaspoon brown sugar

½ teaspoon freshly ground pepper

1 tomato, sliced into thin wedges

6 ounces young or baby *mizuna*

In a shallow bowl large enough to accommodate the steak, stir together all of the marinade ingredients. Add the steak, turn to coat well, and let marinate at room temperature for 30 to 45 minutes. Brush the red onion with the oil and sprinkle with the salt; set aside. Meanwhile, prepare a charcoal grill.

To make the dressing, in a small saucepan over low heat, heat the water. Add the miso and stir to incorporate. Add the mirin, vinegar, tamari or soy sauce, brown sugar, and pepper and mix well. Remove from the heat.

When the coals are hot, place the steak over the hottest coals and the onions to the side over indirect heat. Grill the steak until medium-rare, about 5 minutes per side, keeping an eye on the onions and turning them with tongs as they begin to brown. They are done when they are slightly charred and soft. Transfer the steak and the onions to a chopping board. Thinly slice the steak against the grain. Slice the onion rounds in half.

Rewarm the miso dressing over low heat. In a large bowl, combine the steak, onions, tomato wedges, and *mizuna*. Toss with the warm dressing to wilt the *mizuna* slightly and serve immediately.

芥
菜

mustard cabbage

ALSO KNOWN AS: gai choy *(Cantonese), mustard greens*

The leaves of this hearty green are pungent and spicy, as you might imagine from the name. Two common types exist: The most easily identifiable variety has a uniquely thick, curving, almost bulbous ribbed base where the stems meet the handsome, slightly ruffled leaves. The other variety is called bamboo mustard cabbage (*juk gai choy*), and although it has a similar taste, its stems are straight and thinner, closer to the size of *choy sum*.

mustard cabbage

SELECTING AND STORING: Look for moist, firm stems and leaves with no holes or signs of yellowing. Depending on the variety you have, mustard cabbage can be stored in a loosely closed plastic bag in the refrigerator crisper for up to 5 days, and sometimes longer.

HOW TO USE: Wash well, as grit can get in the spaces around the base of the stems. The bulbous stems of the largest mustard cabbages are traditionally pickled, while younger ones, as well as bamboo mustard cabbage, are used more often in soups and stir-fries.

chinese pickled mustard cabbage

MAKES 1 QUART

The crisp stems and spicy flavor of large mustard cabbage make them great for pickling. Try chopping these semisweet pickles and tossing them with stir-fried shredded pork, adding them to a soup with tofu, or setting them out for everyone to snack on before a meal.

1 pound mustard cabbage

2 tablespoons kosher salt

1½ cups rice vinegar

½ cup sugar

4 slices fresh ginger

4 dried red chilies

Remove only the very top of the leaves of the mustard cabbage. The leaves attached directly to the stalk may remain. Cut the greens into 3-inch lengths and put into a large bowl. Toss with 1 tablespoon of the salt and set aside for 1 hour.

In a saucepan, bring the remaining 1 tablespoon salt, the rice vinegar, and the sugar to a boil. Cook for about 3 minutes or until the sugar dissolves. Add the ginger and chilies and remove from the heat to cool.

Pour off any liquid from the mustard cabbage, and place the cabbage in a clean glass quart jar with a lid. Pour the sugar-and-vinegar mixture over the mustard cabbage, put the lid on the jar, and refrigerate. If the liquid does not completely cover the greens, gently shake the jar on occasion until the greens wilt enough for the liquid to cover them.

The pickled greens should be ready to eat within 2 days and are best enjoyed within 2 weeks.

asian gumbo with mustard cabbage and chinese sausage

SERVES 4

My Louisiana friends would surely cry sacrilege at the thought of Asian gumbo, although the same elements—sausage, mustard greens, and rice—often share a bowl in the South. Don't let the roux stop you. Despite the lore that surrounds this rich, nutty union of flour and oil, it's actually simple to make (just don't stop stirring). If sweet and mild Chinese sausage is unavailable, andouille sausage is a traditional, but much spicier, replacement.

6 tablespoons canola oil

⅓ cup all-purpose flour

1 tablespoon chopped garlic

1 teaspoon chopped fresh ginger

¼ cup chopped shallot

½ cup chopped yellow onion

½ cup chopped green onion, white and green parts

2 Chinese sausages, sliced into coins ¼ inch thick

4 cups chicken broth

½ teaspoon kosher salt

1 to 2 teaspoons cayenne pepper

2 pounds tender young Chinese mustard cabbage, tough ends discarded and stems and leaves cut crosswise into 2-inch pieces

Hot steamed white rice for serving

In a heavy 4-quart pot over medium-low heat, heat the oil. Sprinkle the flour over the oil, all the while stirring with a wooden spoon. Continuing to stir so that the flour doesn't burn, cook the roux for 10 to 12 minutes, or until it is a little darker than peanut butter.

Add the garlic, ginger, shallot, yellow onion, and green onion to the roux and cook for about 5 minutes, or until the vegetables are soft. Add the sausage and cook, stirring, for another 2 to 3 minutes, or until the fat in the sausage is translucent. Add the chicken broth, salt, and cayenne, and bring to a simmer. Add the greens, reduce the heat to low, cover, and cook for 3 to 5 minutes, or until the mustard greens have cooked down.

Remove the cover and continue cooking for another 10 minutes, or until the mustard greens are tender but still vivid in color. Serve in a bowl over rice.

紹
菜

napa cabbage

ALSO KNOWN AS: *Celery cabbage, Chinese cabbage, Peking cabbage*

Napa cabbage has become ubiquitous in Western markets. Lighter and crispier in texture and more peppery in flavor than common green cabbage, the leaves readily absorb whatever flavors you add to it. Although there are different varieties, the kind of napa cabbage you'll see here is usually pale green to white, wrinkled as a walnut, and almost oblong in shape. You might also run across a type that is more cylindrical and with less compact leaves.

napa cabbage

SELECTING AND STORING: Pick up a head of cabbage and hold it in your hand. The heavier it feels, the better. A couple of wilted leaves should pose no problem, but avoid heads that are browning. Napa cabbage can be stored in a loosely closed plastic bag in the refrigerator crisper for a week or more.

HOW TO USE: Remove the first round of outer leaves. I generally carve out the very bottom of the core. There's no end to the ways Napa cabbage can be used. It's crisp and light enough to shred raw and add to salads and hearty enough to be tossed into a soup toward the end of cooking. Koreans ferment enormous quantities of it for kimchi, and it's also used as a wrapper for steaming.

steamed halibut with sweet miso wrapped in cabbage

Steaming is one of the easiest and most healthful ways to cook fish. The fish won't dry out as easily, and there's no grease-spattered mess. This delicately flavored, Japanese-inspired dish uses blanched napa cabbage to wrap the fillets like little gifts, ideal for a first course or light main dish. It's a good idea to blanch more than 8 cabbage leaves, so if one rips, you'll have some on reserve. A sprinkle of slivered green onions makes a nice garnish.

SERVES 4
as a first course

SWEET MISO SAUCE:

6 tablespoons red miso

¼ cup mirin

2 tablespoons sake

2 tablespoons sugar

12 dried shiitake mushrooms, soaked in
    warm water for 30 minutes

1 large head napa cabbage

2½ pounds halibut fillets or other firm white
    fish fillets such as monkfish or sea bass,
    each about 1 inch thick

1-inch piece fresh ginger, peeled and cut
    into matchsticks

6 green onions, white and some green parts,
    cut into matchsticks

To make the sauce, in a small bowl, stir together all of the ingredients and set aside.

Bring a large pot filled with water to a boil. Meanwhile, drain the shiitakes and squeeze out any excess moisture. Remove the hard stems and thinly slice the caps. Set aside.

Carefully separate 16 or more of the largest outer leaves from the head of cabbage, taking care not to tear them. Place a bowl of ice water nearby. Lower the cabbage leaves into the boiling water and

blanch for 1 minute. Remove the cabbage from the water with tongs, rinse briefly in the bowl of ice water to cool, and stack the leaves flat on a plate.

Prepare a bamboo steamer or a metal steamer rack by brushing it with oil. Fill a wok or large pot half full with water and bring to a gentle boil.

Meanwhile, make the cabbage packets: Cut the fish fillets into eight 3-inch squares. (They do not need to be exact.) On a flat surface, crisscross 2 leaves of the blanched cabbage to form an X. (If the stem ends are too thick to be pliable for rolling, use a knife to shave a thin slice off each one.) In the center, place one-eighth of the ginger, green onions, and sliced mushrooms. Coat one side of each piece of fish with about 2 tablespoons of the miso sauce and place the fish, miso side down, on top of the filling. Carefully wrap the fish like a package, bringing the opposite sides of the leaves up and over until securely closed. (You can use a toothpick to hold the leaves in place, if necessary.) Place the package, seal-side down, in the bamboo steamer or on the metal steamer rack. Repeat with the remaining pieces of fish and filling.

Position the steamer above the water, cover, and steam for 10 to 15 minutes, or until the fish is no longer translucent. Using a spatula, gently remove the packages, serving each diner 2 packages. Pass the extra miso sauce at the table to pour over the top.

sesame pork skewers with kimchi

No Korean meal is complete without kimchi, an addictively pungent relish spiked with loads of garlic and Korean red pepper flakes (which, along with Korean hot-pepper paste, are worth searching out). Although kimchi can be made with everything from cucumbers to bean sprouts, the most common version features napa cabbage. Kimchi takes at least 4 days to ferment, so don't forget to plan ahead. Add Soybean Sprouts with Sesame and Garlic (page 50), Jap Chae (page 26), and bowls of steamed short-grain white rice to the meal, and you will have laid out a worthy Korean spread.

SERVES 4

KIMCHI:

1 head napa cabbage, about 2 ½ pounds, quartered,
    cored, and chopped into 2-inch pieces

3 tablespoons kosher salt

½ cup shredded daikon

2 teaspoons finely chopped garlic

1 tablespoon finely chopped fresh ginger

6 green onions, white part finely chopped and
    green part cut into 1-inch pieces

2 to 3 tablespoons Korean red pepper flakes

1 tablespoon sugar

1 tablespoon soy sauce

1 tablespoon distilled white vinegar

SESAME PORK:

2 teaspoons finely chopped garlic

2 tablespoons Korean hot-pepper paste

½ teaspoon Korean red pepper flakes

2 teaspoons sugar

2 tablespoons soy sauce

1 tablespoon toasted sesame seeds

1 pound boneless pork chops, sliced on the diagonal
    into strips 3 ½ inches long by ¼ inch thick
    (24 strips total)

6 green onions, each trimmed to 3 inches

2 tablespoons canola oil

To make the kimchi, in a large bowl, combine the cabbage and the salt. Set aside for 3 hours or for up to overnight. Turn the cabbage into a colander to drain off all the liquid that accumulated, pressing down firmly with your fist. Return the cabbage to the bowl.

Add all of the remaining ingredients to the cabbage and stir well to combine. Pack the mixture into clean glass pint jars with lids, pushing down on it to rid it of any excess air pockets. Screw on the lids and refrigerate for 4 days before eating. It will keep for at least a month, depending on how fermented you like it.

To make the pork, in a bowl, combine the garlic, pepper paste, pepper flakes, sugar, soy sauce, and sesame seeds. Mix well to form a paste. Add the pork to it and mix well. Marinate for at least 30 minutes or for up to 2 hours at room temperature.

Thread 2 pieces of pork onto a wooden skewer, piercing each piece, through the top, middle, and end. Follow with a green onion, pierced on the diagonal. Follow with 2 more pieces of pork. Thread 5 more skewers in the same way.

In a wide, shallow skillet over medium-high heat, heat the oil. Place the skewers in the skillet and cook for 3 to 5 minutes on each side, until the pork is just cooked through but not dry. Transfer to a platter and serve with the kimchi on the side.

japanese "as you like it" pancakes

At okonomiyaki *restaurants in Japan, everyone feasts on these fat vegetable pancakes. Customers can make their own at griddle-topped tables, or sit at narrow counters, order from a long list of ingredients, and watch a cook make the pancakes for them. Admittedly, I've only had these pancakes at Japanese restaurants in the States, but it's also a great way to use up leftovers at home. Try mixing other vegetables into the pancakes such as corn, peas, bean sprouts, or chopped daikon. Alternative dipping sauces include hot Chinese mustard or 1/2 cup soy sauce sweetened with a few tablespoons of sugar. Nori, dried seaweed sheets also known as laver, is easily found at Japanese markets and some mainstream grocery stores. It is commonly used as a wrapper for sushi and is sold both plain and toasted.*

SERVES 4

DIPPING SAUCE:

1/4 cup ketchup

1 tablespoon plus 2 teaspoons Worcestershire sauce

1/4 teaspoon dry mustard

2 tablespoons sake

1 teaspoon tamari or soy sauce

PANCAKES:

3 eggs

2/3 cup chicken broth or water

1/3 cup all-purpose flour

2 teaspoons tamari or soy sauce

1/4 teaspoon kosher salt

1 1/2 cups finely chopped napa cabbage

1/2 cup chopped red onion

1 serrano chili, finely chopped

2 tablespoons canola oil

3/4 cup diced cooked chicken, pork, or shrimp, or
   a combination

Toasted nori seaweed, crumbled (optional)

Toasted white or black sesame seeds (optional)

To make the dipping sauce, in a small bowl, combine all of the ingredients and mix well.

To make the pancakes, in a bowl, whisk the eggs until blended. Whisk in the broth, then gradually whisk in the flour. Add the tamari or soy sauce and salt and stir in the cabbage, onion, and chili.

Over medium-low heat, heat a large cast-iron skillet or heavy nonstick skillet. Brush on the oil or pour it in and tilt to coat the bottom of the pan evenly. Pour in the egg mixture and immediately sprinkle your choice of chicken, pork, or shrimp (or a combination) evenly on top. Smooth the surface with a spatula. Cook for about 5 minutes, or until the underside is nicely browned. Use the spatula to cut the pancake into equal wedges, and carefully turn each section (having 2 spatulas helps). Cook for about 5 minutes more, or until browned on the second side.

Divide the pancake wedges among 4 plates. Sprinkle with the nori and sesame seeds, if desired. Serve at once and pass the dipping sauce at the table.

豆
苗

pea sprouts and pea shoots

ALSO KNOWN AS: dau miu *(Cantonese)*

The curling tendrils and leaves of the snow pea plant (often a variety cultivated specifically for its shoots), pea shoots taste like the essence of a young pea eaten fresh from its pod. They are sold in two stages. Pea sprouts, no taller than a couple inches, are often found prepackaged in plastic bags, and are available off and on year-round. The big pea shoots are the real extravagance though. They're strictly seasonal, arriving in the markets in the early spring.

pea sprouts and pea shoots

SELECTING AND STORING: If pea sprouts are sold in a plastic bag, make sure they haven't been crushed. When purchasing pea shoots, look for the most fragile ones you can find. Even slightly wilted shoots are preferable to tough leaves. You'll find the more expensive ones are generally only the most tender tips. Pea shoots are best eaten the day of their purchase.

HOW TO USE: Some people stir-fry pea sprouts, but I prefer them raw in a salad or lightly dressed, a bundle set atop grilled fish. Preparing pea shoots, on the other hand, can be laborious. It's crucial to pinch off just the most tender tendrils from the tops and remove any part of the stem that's remotely woody or tough. This process will diminish the bulk of the pea shoots quite a bit, so it's best to start out with far more than you might think you will need. Pea shoots are best prepared simply, so that their gentle sweetness isn't lost. Stir-fry them quickly with garlic, or let them wilt in the hot broth of a delicate seafood soup.

salad of pea sprouts, satsumas, and beets with ginger-mint dressing

At Dine, one of my favorite San Francisco restaurants, chef Julia McClaskey serves a fantastic salad of pea sprouts with jewels of beets and bites of creamy goat cheese that inspired the idea for this recipe. I've added Satsumas (although sectioned navel oranges would work fine), a type of mandarin orange introduced to the States from Japan over a century ago. Sweet and almost seedless, this special citrus is the one I look forward to every fall. To grate the ginger for the dressing, use a ginger grater or even a small-holed cheese grater, reserving the juice. Double the dressing, and keep some on hand for the week.

SERVES 4

GINGER DRESSING:

1 tablespoon grated fresh ginger, plus juice (see recipe introduction)

2 tablespoons chopped fresh mint

¼ cup canola oil

7 tablespoons rice vinegar

1 teaspoon sugar

Kosher salt and white pepper to taste

4 beets

½ cup water

6 ounces pea sprouts

2 Satsuma mandarin oranges, peeled and sectioned

To make the dressing, in a jar with a lid, combine all the ingredients. Shake well and set aside until needed.

To roast the beets, preheat the oven to 400°F. Trim the stems, leaving about ½ inch intact, but do not peel. Place the beets in a small roasting pan, add the water, cover with aluminum foil, and bake for 45 to 60 minutes, or until the beets are tender when pierced with a knife. Remove from the oven, let cool, and then slip off the skins and cut the beets into small wedges.

In a large bowl, gently toss together the beets, pea sprouts, and Satsuma sections. Shake the dressing again to reincorporate. Toss the salad with the dressing and serve.

big pea shoots stir-fried with garlic

The key to a tasty platter of pea shoots, as with all delicate greens, is a hot wok and quick moves. Don't be lazy and overflow the wok with your carefully trimmed shoots, just to watch the top bunch sit there unfazed while the bottom cooks to death (I know this from experience). Set the table first, as these are best the minute they are done.

1 tablespoon Shaoxing wine

¼ cup chicken broth or water

2 teaspoons soy sauce

¼ teaspoon sugar

2 tablespoons canola oil

2 tablespoons finely chopped garlic

1 pound big pea shoots, trimmed to the tender tips

2 teaspoons cornstarch dissolved in 4 teaspoons water

In a small bowl, combine the Shaoxing wine, chicken broth or water, soy sauce, and sugar. Set near the stove.

In a wok or large, deep skillet over medium-high heat, heat the oil. Add the garlic and stir-fry for 15 seconds until fragrant. Add the pea shoots and toss to coat with the oil and garlic. Raise the heat to high and add the sauce mixture. Stir-fry the pea shoots for 15 seconds, cover, and cook for another minute, or until wilted. Uncover, add the cornstarch mixture, and stir-fry another 30 seconds, or until the sauce has thickened. Turn out onto a platter and serve at once.

tatsoi

ALSO KNOWN AS: *flat cabbage, rosette bok choy, rosette* pak choy

The *mesclun,* or spring mix, craze has introduced us to a lot of greens we had never before seen on our plates, and *tatsoi* is one of them. This brassica grows in a rosette, sometimes flat against the ground, and has crinkled, dark green leaves and often a white stem, much like that of bok choy, to which it's related. In Western markets, *tatsoi,* its Japanese name, is the most common labeling, and I've found that Japanese markets sometimes carry it in its mature stage. To find it young and loose, try a good farmers' market or gourmet superstore—or at a restaurant, where it's likely to be the bed for your sea bass.

tatsoi

SELECTING AND STORING: Store *tatsoi* in a loosely closed plastic bag in the refrigerator crisper up to 5 days.

HOW TO USE: In its baby stage, *tatsoi* is nice raw tossed with slices of Asian pear and toasted pecans. It also is good wilted in a salad. If you find it in its mature stage, be sure to wash it particularly well to remove any of the trapped grit that results from growing so close to the ground. Try it quickly stir-fried with ginger and go from there.

water spinach

ALSO KNOWN AS: kang kong *(Malay), morning glory,* ong choy *(Cantonese), swamp cabbage*

Water spinach is impressive to behold. Sold in tall, leafy bundles that can barely be contained by the pink plastic bags every Chinatown market seems to use, it has long, flat arrow-shaped leaves and thin, hollow stems. Despite the name, it is not related to spinach (it is closer botanically to the sweet potato), and it is cultivated both in waterways and in fields. Water spinach is valued for its crunchy stems, which contrast nicely with the leaves' slightly slippery texture and mild flavor when cooked. The Vietnamese, serious fans of the vegetable, sometimes split the pale green stems lengthwise and soak them in water, which makes them curl into little corkscrews used for decoration.

water spinach

SELECTING AND STORING: The leaves of water spinach fade quickly, so look for a particularly perky bunch. You can store it in a loosely closed plastic bag in the refrigerator for a couple of days at the most. Wrap whatever leaves are sticking out with a damp towel.

HOW TO USE: Remove the fibrous part of the stems, usually about an inch or two below the last leaves. Before cooking, pinch or cut the water spinach into 2-inch pieces. Although it can be eaten raw, water spinach is better briefly blanched, taking into consideration that it will cook down to at least one-third of its size. It looks rather stringy when cooked, but if prepared correctly it's very good. The Japanese use it to make *ohitashi* (a cold salad that often calls for spinach), but it's also traditionally stir-fried with big flavors: lots of garlic, pungent shrimp paste, fragrant Thai chilies, or fermented bean curd.

Hannah An's water spinach with cherry tomatoes and shrimp

SERVES 4
as a side dish

In this recipe, Hannah separates the stems of the water spinach from the leaves, a process that is tedious if you don't have the time and meditative if you do. The alternative is to cut the stems into 2-inch pieces, leaves and all.

1 pound water spinach, stems trimmed to where the leaves start

10 cherry tomatoes, halved crosswise

1 tablespoon fish sauce

2 teaspoons fresh lime juice

1 tablespoon sugar

1 tablespoon canola oil

2 teaspoons minced garlic

1 tablespoon minced shallot

1 tablespoon crab paste, or 2 teaspoons shrimp paste

½ pound large shrimp, peeled and deveined

1 cup bean sprouts, blanched 10 seconds and well drained (optional)

2 teaspoons toasted sesame seeds

Separate the leaves from the stems of the water spinach and cut the stems into 2-inch pieces. Bring a large pot of water to a boil. Add the water spinach, first the stems and 15 seconds later the leaves. Cook for 1 minute total and drain in a colander. Rinse with cold water and drain well. Set aside.

Place a strainer over a bowl, hold each tomato half over the strainer and squeeze to force out the seed sacs and juice. Set aside the tomatoes, and press the tomato juice through the strainer. Add the fish sauce, lime juice, and sugar to the juice.

In a wok or large, deep skillet over high heat, heat the oil. Add the garlic, shallot, and crab or shrimp paste and stir-fry for 1 minute, or until fragrant. Add the shrimp and stir-fry until opaque. Add the tomato halves, water spinach, the bean sprouts, if using. Add the fish sauce mixture, and toss.

Transfer to a platter and sprinkle with the sesame seeds. Serve at once or at room temperature.

Hannah An on **water spinach**

Hannah An runs Thang Long, one of the oldest Vietnamese restaurants in San Francisco and a destination famous for its roast Dungeness crab. Her family also owns Crustacean, a restaurant that draws stars in both its Beverly Hills and San Francisco locations.

One of Hannah's favorite vegetables is water spinach, or *ong choy* (the Cantonese name) as she calls it. "*Ong choy* is as common in Vietnam as spinach is here," says Hannah. "You see it growing all over the countryside." After Hannah blanches the vegetable, she chills the water she used to cook it, adds a squeeze of lemon, and drinks it. "It's supposed to be good for your skin, and it's really soothing. You can also add a tomato to the broth." Hannah recommends using your judgment when picking out water spinach, looking for young, tender stems and leaves.

two

roots, shoots, and bulbs

Not the most handsome or colorful group, these vegetables barely see the light of day before they're plucked from the ground and rushed to the market. With the exception of bean sprouts and daikon, many of these may be unfamiliar to the Western cook. From the crunch of bamboo shoots to the creaminess of taro, they are vegetables primarily used for their texture, a characteristic valued in Asian cooking almost as much as taste. Unadorned, they may lack pizzazz, but if you know how to dress them up, you've got a date.

roots, shoots, and bulbs

bamboo shoots

Fresh bamboo shoots can be hard to come by, even in Asian markets. If you find them, keep in mind that two types are common: spring (fatter) and winter (slimmer and considered more desirable). Bamboo shoots have an outer husk that must be removed before you get to the edible core, which then must be boiled to remove the toxic hydrocyanic acid before it can be eaten. For these reasons, I don't use fresh bamboo shoots and recommend sticking with the processed ones that are sold in tubs of water (their conelike shape reminds me of little beehives) or the canned ones, boiling them for a minute to remove any bitter flavor before using. Bamboo shoots are used in stir-fries, curries, and soups. Try them braised with pork and ginger or sliced thinly and stir-fried with scallops and green onions.

bamboo shoot

bean sprouts mung bean, soybean

The Asian cook relies primarily on two kinds of bean sprouts: mung bean (usually known as bean sprouts) and the nutritious soybean, identifiable by the yellow head at one end and its larger size. Mung bean sprouts are the smaller white sprouts sold in every Western market. Both kinds are appreciated for their crisp and succulent texture, but nutty-flavored soybean sprouts stand much better on their own. You'll find both types sold in heaping piles and prepackaged in plastic bags.

bean sprouts (soy and mung)

SELECTING AND STORING: Look for crisp, white bean sprouts that aren't too stringy, an indication that they're old. If the pile of sprouts you have to choose from looks a bit handled and broken into bits, ask the grocer if he or she has fresh ones stored in the back. Bean sprouts are perishable, but you can keep them in an airtight plastic container (it protects them from getting banged up) in the refrigerator for 2 to 3 days.

HOW TO USE: The most diligent cooks will pinch off the heads and tails of mung bean sprouts (just the tails are removed from soybean sprouts). Although it does affect the texture slightly, the main reason for this step is aesthetic, and I usually choose to skip it. Mung bean sprouts can be eaten raw, but soybean sprouts are rumored to be slightly toxic uncooked. Either way, I find that blanching both types for a few seconds and immediately refreshing them in cold water removes a faint bitter taste. They are then ready to be used in everything from stir-fries to soups to salads.

pad thai

Present a group with a four-page-long American-style Thai menu, and I guarantee someone will zero in on pad Thai. *You'll find that, made at home, this beloved noodle dish yields much lighter flavors than you'll get at a restaurant. Many recipes call for ketchup, but I prefer to use tamarind and sugar for a more subtle sweet-tart taste. To make it vegetarian, replace the shrimp with ½-inch cubes of fried firm tofu.*

SERVES 4

½ pound flat dried rice noodles

¼ cup fish sauce

3 tablespoons tamarind concentrate

1 teaspoon sugar

1 tablespoon fresh lime juice

½ cup chicken broth

3 tablespoons canola oil

2 teaspoons finely chopped garlic

¼ cup finely chopped shallot

1 teaspoon chili sauce such as *sambal oelek*

½ pound shrimp, peeled and deveined

2 eggs, lightly beaten

2 cups mung bean sprouts

½ cup chopped fresh cilantro

½ cup diagonally sliced green onion, white and green parts

½ cup chopped unsalted roasted peanuts

1 lime, quartered

Place the noodles in a bowl with hot water to cover and let soak for 20 minutes.

Meanwhile, stir together the fish sauce, tamarind, sugar, lime juice, and chicken broth and set aside.

In a large wok or large, deep skillet over high heat, heat 2 tablespoons of the oil. Add the garlic, shallot, and chili sauce and stir-fry for 30 seconds, or until fragrant. Add the shrimp and continue to stir-fry for 3 to 5 minutes, or until the shrimp are opaque. Transfer to a plate and set aside.

Add the remaining 1 tablespoon oil to the wok. When the oil is hot, add the eggs and stir-fry quickly until barely scrambled. Add the fish sauce mixture and cook for about 3 minutes, or until the eggs have just set. Drain the noodles and add to the pan along with the bean sprouts and the reserved shrimp. Using a spatula or fork in each hand, toss to combine. Continue to cook and toss for another 1 to 2 minutes, or until the noodles are soft but chewy.

Transfer the noodles to a platter and garnish with the cilantro, green onion, and peanuts. Serve with the lime wedges.

soybean sprouts with sesame and garlic

SERVES 4
as a side dish

This addictively crunchy dish was part of a feast that a Korean friend's mother made for me one day. She served it along with sautéed skewered beef, slippery, transparent blocks of mung bean paste that had been thinly sliced and seasoned, and five different types of chili-red kimchi. Unlike a lot of Korean recipes, salt is used here in place of soy sauce, so that the sprouts retain their whiteness.

¾ pound soybean sprouts

1 tablespoon sesame oil

1 teaspoon finely chopped garlic

1 teaspoon kosher salt

1 green onion, green part only, matchstick-cut
 lengthwise into 2-inch pieces

2 teaspoons toasted sesame seeds

Bring a large pot of water to a boil, add the soybean sprouts, and blanch for 10 seconds. Drain in a colander, rinse with cold water, and shake out any excess water.

Transfer the blanched sprouts to a bowl. Add the sesame oil, garlic, salt, green onion, and sesame seeds and toss gently to mix well. Serve at room temperature.

daikon

ALSO KNOWN AS: *Chinese turnip, icicle radish,* lo bok *(Cantonese),* mooli *(Indian), white radish*

Many Asian cuisines, from Vietnamese to Indian, make use of this long, thick radish, but it is most commonly known by its Japanese name, daikon. There are many different varieties. The one you'll commonly find in Western markets looks something like an overgrown smooth white carrot, while Asian markets often carry examples that range from fat to skinny, and in colors from green-and-white to red (although I've never come across the latter here). Available in most supermarkets, daikon is cheap, sturdy, and long lasting. Its slightly spicy but relatively mild radish flavor is as pleasant raw as stewed.

daikon (white and green-and-white)

SELECTING AND STORING: Similar to any root, daikon should feel heavy for its size and firm in your hand. The skin should be smooth and unblemished. Store it in a well-sealed plastic bag in the refrigerator for 1 to 2 weeks.

HOW TO USE: Daikon should be peeled before used, but that's the only rule of thumb. Shred it raw to add to a salad or an Indian *raita*, serve it as part of a crudité plate, or braise it in place of parsnips in a stew. The Chinese make a pudding out of daikon, the Vietnamese make daikon cakes, the Japanese finely grate it and add it to dipping sauces, and the Koreans consider it a standard component of kimchi. My only advice is don't leave it cut up and uncovered in your refrigerator for too long. It can give off a pungent smell.

shredded daikon and carrot salad with mustard seeds

SERVES 4
as a side dish

In teaching me the ways of Indian home cooking, my friend Sona Rao devised this simple and refreshing salad. All white, orange, and green and dotted with brown mustard seeds, it makes a pretty addition to any Indian meal. Serve it on the side, or spoon it over fish like a relish.

1 daikon, about 1 pound, peeled and grated
   (about 3 cups)
2 carrots, peeled and grated (about ½ cup)
¼ cup chopped fresh cilantro
4 teaspoons fresh lemon juice
1 teaspoon sugar
½ teaspoon kosher salt
1 tablespoon canola oil
2 teaspoons brown mustard seeds

In a bowl, combine the daikon, carrots, cilantro, lemon juice, sugar, and salt. Allow to sit for 15 to 30 minutes, so that the flavors combine and the juices drain. Pour off any accumulated liquid.

In a small pan over medium heat, heat the oil. Add the mustard seeds, cover with a lid, and fry for about 15 seconds until the seeds quit popping (they will sound like teeny popcorn popping away). Take care not to let the mustard seeds burn. Immediately pour the mustard seeds and hot oil over the salad and stir to combine. Serve at room temperature.

Barbara Tropp's steamed salmon on daikon with fresh cilantro pesto

SERVES 4

My worn copy of Barbara's China Moon Cookbook *practically opens itself to this recipe, now spattered with stains. This is my simplified version.*

CILANTRO PESTO:

2 cups packed chopped fresh cilantro leaves
   and stems

¼ cup pine nuts, toasted

1½ teaspoons minced garlic

2½ teaspoons fresh lemon juice

1 teaspoon kosher salt

1 teaspoon chili oil

1 teaspoon sesame oil

Sesame oil for brushing

¼ pound daikon, peeled and cut into paper-thin
   rounds

2 pounds salmon fillet, cut into 4 equal portions

2 tablespoons peeled and fine-matchstick-cut
   fresh ginger

To make the pesto, in a food processor or blender, combine the cilantro, pine nuts, and garlic and process to a paste. With the machine running, add the lemon juice and salt. Combine the chili oil and sesame oil and, again with the machine running, add in a thin stream, processing until the pesto has emulsified. If it's too thick, blend in a bit of warm water to obtain a rich, pourable consistency. (If working in advance, cover with a piece of plastic wrap pressed directly on the surface and refrigerate. Bring to room temperature before using.)

Fill a wok or steamer half-full with water and bring to a rapid boil. Meanwhile, choose a heatproof plate that is an inch or so smaller in diameter than your bamboo steamer or steamer rack. Brush the plate with the sesame oil and place in the steamer or rack. Arrange the daikon on the plate in concentric circles, overlapping the rounds, to make a bed for the fish. Place the fish fillets in a single layer on top, and scatter the ginger evenly over all.

Position the steamer over the boiling water, cover, and steam over high heat for 10 to 12 minutes per inch of thickness, or until a knife tip inserted in the thickest portion of the fish shows it to be medium to well done (depending on how you like it).

Promptly transfer the daikon and fish to plates. Top the fish with a broad band of pesto and serve.

Barbara Tropp on **Daikon**

Barbara Tropp, author of *The Modern Art of Chinese Cooking* and *China Moon Cookbook,* whizzing in and out of Chinese markets and chatting effortlessly in Mandarin to one purveyor and inquiring about the water chestnuts in English to the next, is a sight to behold. Barbara holds daikon in high regard for its versatility. "It's not only delicious—it's the be all and end all for vegetable carving. The last time I was in China, I watched chefs carve daikon into white cranes and spider chrysanthemums, both symbols of longevity," she recalls in wonder. "The hot pink daikon and pale green ones are made into elaborate flowers like peonies, roses, and tulips."

When Barbara selects a daikon, she looks at the stem end to see how recently it has been harvested. She knows that produce workers in Western markets often lop off both ends. If this is the case, just make sure the daikon is firm and slimmer rather than fatter (if it is of the long variety). She likes to pickle daikon with lemon, chilies, and ginger, and regularly uses it as a bed for steaming.

蓮
藕

lotus root

Lotus root is unique to the Asian culinary world. More accurately a rhizome, its buff-colored sausagelike links are typically sold in twos and threes. Although often already cleaned, sometimes you'll find it still coated in the mud in which it grows. The ugly duckling of Asian vegetables, it is not a pretty sight until it's sliced crosswise, when it reveals a beautiful and distinctive pattern, like a paper snowflake. The flavor and crisp texture is reminiscent of jicama, but it can taste more astringent.

lotus root

SELECTING AND STORING: Look for unbruised, unblemished skin and a fresh smell. Although I usually see lotus root sold unpackaged, some Asian supermarkets display the single links scrubbed clean and vacuum packed. Store it uncut in a loosely sealed plastic bag in the refrigerator for up to 2 weeks.

HOW TO USE: Lotus root needs to be washed well to remove any mud, and the skin must be peeled. To keep it from browning, immediately put cut pieces into water with a squeeze of lemon. Even when cooked for quite a while, it maintains its crisp texture. It is eaten blanched in salads, stuffed, chopped up and stir-fried, pickled, and candied. The lacy slices make beautiful Japanese tempura and are perfect for floating in a brothy soup.

miso soup with lotus root, leeks, and tofu

SERVES 4
as a first course

Miso soup invites any number of vegetable combinations: Try adding green beans, cabbage, turnips, bamboo shoots, daikon, or spinach. Dashi, a delicate Japanese fish stock, is easy to make: Bring one 2-inch piece of konbu (a type of kelp) and 4 cups of water to a simmer. Add ¼ cup bonito flakes (dried fish flakes), and remove from the heat. Let stand for 1 minute and strain. The dashi is now ready to use. The kelp and the fish flakes can be found in Japanese markets.

4 cups dashi, chicken broth, or water

1 large leek, halved lengthwise, rinsed thoroughly, and thinly sliced

1 carrot, peeled, halved lengthwise, and thinly sliced

5 dried shiitake mushrooms, soaked in warm water for 30 minutes, drained, stemmed, and thinly sliced

16 thin slices peeled lotus root

¼ pound tofu, cut into ½-inch cubes

2 to 3 tablespoons red miso

2 green onions, white and green parts, thinly sliced

In a saucepan over medium heat, bring the dashi, chicken broth, or water to a simmer. Add the leek, carrot, shiitake mushrooms, and lotus root and simmer for 2 to 3 minutes, or until the carrots are slightly tender. Add the tofu. In a small bowl, dissolve the miso in a little of the hot broth, and then add to the soup. Taste the broth and add more miso, if necessary, stirring to combine. Add the green onions and serve.

Grace Young's fragrant lotus root salad

SERVES 4
as a first course

This recipe calls for briefly blanching the lotus root, keeping it crisp yet removing the raw taste. The salad is refreshing, with its mixture of salty, sweet, sour, nutty, and peppery flavors.

1 large section lotus root, about ½ pound

Boiling water as needed

2 teaspoons thin soy sauce

2 teaspoons Chinese red rice vinegar

2 teaspoons sesame oil

1 teaspoon sugar

½ teaspoon salt

¼ teaspoon white pepper

Using a vegetable peeler, peel the lotus root. With a chef's knife, cut off the rootlike strands, then rinse the root under cold water. Cut it in half lengthwise and rinse again to remove any mud still lodged in the root. Thinly slice the lotus root into ⅛-inch-thick half-moons. Rinse again in case there is any mud. Place the lotus root in a heatproof bowl and pour in enough boiling water to cover the lotus root completely. Set aside for 5 minutes. Rinse under cold water, drain, and pat dry.

In a medium bowl, stir together the soy sauce, vinegar, sesame oil, sugar, salt, and pepper. Add the drained lotus root and toss to combine. Refrigerate for about 1 hour, or serve at room temperature.

Grace Young on **lotus root**

When I asked Grace Young, the author of the beautifully written memoir and Cantonese cookbook *The Wisdom of the Chinese Kitchen*, which Asian vegetable meant the most to her, she answered without batting an eye: "Lotus root. What other vegetable is regarded as a sacred symbol in Buddhist culture?" Grown in mud, the lotus flower emerges ivory colored and pure, and every part of the plant is used by the Chinese in cooking. The blossom is enjoyed for its sheer beauty, the leaves are used to wrap food for cooking, and the seeds and stalk carry medicinal value. When the rhizome is dried, it is ground for flour. According to Grace, the fresh "root" is the most versatile part, equally delicious in stir-fries, soups (where it is known for its blood tonic properties), and even in salads.

When Grace selects lotus root, she looks for one with three links. "The large section is best for stir-fries," she says, "while the two smaller sections are typically used for soups." She also looks for those with a fresh, clean smell and a solid, heavy feel in the hand.

taro root

This tuber, an Asian pantry staple, is not relegated to Asian cuisine by any means. It is a mainstay in parts of Africa and Polynesia and, of course, in Hawaii, where it is made into poi. It tastes slightly nutty-sweet and gets creamy—almost glutinous— when cooked. You'll come across two kinds in the market: small (about the size of a new potato) and large (which can reach up to two pounds and has purple-flecked flesh). Both have brown, hairy skin and rings that circle in regular intervals.

taro root

SELECTING AND STORING: Inspect taro closely to make sure that it's free of mold and soft spots. Store it in the refrigerator or a cool, dry place for up to a week or more.

HOW TO USE: Much like a potato, taro is not edible until it is cooked, but it is a star mashed or fried. Large taro must be peeled before cooking, while the smaller tubers are often boiled in their skin before being popped out to eat. Although I've never found it to be true, the flesh can irritate some people's skin, and you might want to use gloves when handling it. Taro is used in dim sum to make savory dumplings, but it is also made into sweets such as ice cream and custard. Try cutting it into cubes and throwing them into a coconut soup.

crisp taro pancakes with hoisin-lime dipping sauce

SERVES 8
as an appetizer

Unlike potato pancakes, where you spend half of the time squeezing out the water from the shredded potato, taro fries up like a dream. For passed hors d'oeuvres, try making these pancakes about 2 inches in diameter. The dipping sauce is nice to put out for a party, but I love these cakes even more with a squeeze of lemon and a generous sprinkle of salt. Makes about sixteen 3-inch cakes.

DIPPING SAUCE:

2 tablespoons hoisin sauce

2 tablespoons plus 2 teaspoons fresh lime juice
    (about 3 limes)

2 tablespoons rice vinegar

1 teaspoon sesame oil

1 large taro root, about 1 pound, peeled

Peanut oil for frying

Kosher salt for sprinkling

Toasted sesame seeds for sprinkling

To make the dipping sauce, combine all of the ingredients in a bowl and mix well. Set aside.

Using the large holes of a handheld grater, shred the taro root onto a plate. Scoop up about 2 table-spoons, and pat firmly with your hands (almost twisting the taro between your palms) to make a pancake as thin as possible, about ¼ inch thick, and 3 inches in diameter. It's okay if some of the shreds stick out. Set aside on a platter. Continue making the pancakes until all the taro is used up, stacking them on the platter and using waxed paper between the layers. This step can be done up to 30 minutes ahead of time.

Pour oil to a depth of about 2 inches into a wok or large, deep skillet. Place over high heat and heat until the oil registers 325°F on a deep-frying thermometer, or until a shred of taro dropped into the oil immediately scoots across the surface and sizzles. If the oil is smoking, it is too hot. Adjust the heat as necessary as you go along. Place a few taro cakes in the oil, taking care not to crowd the pan, and fry on one side for 45 to 60 seconds, or until the edges are golden brown. Turn with tongs or a slot-ted spatula and continue to cook on the second side for about 1 minute longer, until golden brown. (The center will always be a bit lighter than the edges.) Transfer to a platter lined with paper towels. Sprinkle generously with salt and sesame seeds.

Serve the first batch immediately with the dipping sauce and continue to fry the remaining taro pancakes.

Kasma Loha-unchit's mashed taro with green onions

SERVES 4

Although it's not technically "mashed," this vegetarian dish is as comforting as mashed potatoes. The only difference is that taro easily breaks down into a distinctly rich, creamy texture that needs no butter and cream. Try serving it alongside Braised Short Ribs with Hearts of Bok Choy (Page 18).

1 large taro root, about 1½ pounds

3 tablespoons peanut oil

2 tablespoons chopped garlic

1½ cups hot water, or as needed

2 tablespoons soy sauce

3 green onions, white and green parts, thinly sliced

With a sharp knife, peel the taro root, quarter it lengthwise, and cut the quarters crosswise into pieces about ¼ inch thick. Set aside.

Heat a wok or a large, heavy pot over high heat. Add the oil and swirl to coat the surface. When the oil is hot, add the garlic and stir. After a few seconds, add the taro and stir to coat it with the oil. Cook until lightly browned, about 3 minutes. Add enough hot water to almost cover the taro. Bring to a boil, reduce the heat to medium, cover, and cook, stirring occasionally to prevent sticking and burning and adding more water if the taro dries out or is still firm. The taro is ready in 20 to 30 minutes, when it breaks down into a creamy mass.

Stir in the soy sauce and green onions and continue to stir until the taro is relatively smooth (some lumps are fine). If necessary, make the taro creamier by adding more water. Cook for about 2 minutes longer to blend the flavor of the green onions with the taro. Transfer to a bowl and serve immediately.

Kasma Loha-unchit on **taro**

When I talk to Kasma Loha-unchit about the taro fritters sold on the street in Thailand, I can almost taste their crisp-creaminess, hot out of the oil. A fantastic Thai cooking teacher and cookbook author, Kasma runs her school out of the small kitchen of her Oakland home half of the year, leads tours of Thailand the remaining months, and is the author of two of my favorite Thai cookbooks, *It Rains Fishes* and *Dancing Shrimp*. Although she grew up outside of Bangkok, her grandparents were Chinese, and this comforting recipe comes from them. "It's just easy country cooking," says Kasma, who uses the large taro for this recipe. "The small ones don't get as smooth and creamy." To keep the taro from irritating your skin after you've handled it, Kasma suggests drying your hands over the stove before you rinse them—a trick her mother taught her.

water chestnuts

Fresh water chestnuts taste nothing like the flavorless imposters you get in a can. Eaten raw, they're delightfully crisp, sweet, and milky, almost like a cross between coconut and jicama. An aquatic vegetable (technically, a corm) grown in ponds or rice paddies, the water chestnut shares only two characteristics with its tree-grown namesake: glossy—although often still muddy—dark brown skin and a nutlike shape that ends in a point. In Asian markets, water chestnuts are usually displayed in boxes in bulk, but like many things, I've also seen them vacuum packed. Although not typically found in Western produce sections, the secret must be leaking out. They've been popping up in my local supermarket.

water chestnuts

SELECTING AND STORING: Look for firm water chestnuts with no sign of wrinkling or soft spots. Store unwashed water chestnuts in the refrigerator in a plastic bag with holes or a paper bag for up to 2 to 3 weeks.

HOW TO USE: Peel water chestnuts with a paring knife, remove all bruises or brown spots, and rinse to remove any remaining mud. Unless you're using them right away, it's best to drop peeled water chestnuts into water with a squirt of lemon to prevent browning. Water chestnuts keep their crisp texture when cooked. They add that little sweet crunch to wonton fillings and make a good match with shrimp or scallops in stir-fries. I also like them barely blanched and added to salads and salsas.

ground pork and water chestnuts in lettuce cups

In Asian cooking, iceberg lettuce is tossed into soups and stir-fries like you would any vegetable. Here it's used in two ways, as an ingredient and as a wrapping. Iceberg is prone to tearing, so if you're worried about imperfect "cups," butter lettuce or red leaf lettuce is a better bet. Personally, I don't think anything can match the crisp and cooling qualities of iceberg, so I look for small, well-formed heads of iceberg, and buy two just to be safe. As a nontraditional alternative, try using radicchio leaves for the "cups." They are just the right size for a first course and add a nice bit of color.

SERVES 8
as a first course

¼ cup bean sauce or black bean–garlic sauce

1 teaspoon sugar

1 teaspoon chili sauce such as *sambal oelek*

1 tablespoon rice vinegar

2 large heads iceberg lettuce

1 tablespoon vegetable oil

1 teaspoon finely chopped garlic

1 pound ground pork

10 fresh water chestnuts, peeled and finely chopped

¼ cup chopped green garlic chives

In a small bowl, stir together the bean sauce, sugar, chili sauce, and rice vinegar and set aside.

Using a paring knife, core each head of lettuce. Separate the roundest outer leaves from each head, taking care not to tear them. You should have at least 8 nicely formed "cups." Gently wash, pat dry, and set aside. Using a knife, finely shred enough of the remaining lettuce to make 1 cup.

In a wok or large, deep skillet over medium-high heat, heat the oil. Cook the garlic for 15 seconds until fragrant. Add the ground pork, breaking it up with a spatula as much as possible, and cook, stirring, for about 5 minutes, or until the meat is no longer pink. Drain off any fat.

Return the pan to medium heat. Add the bean sauce mixture and stir to mix well. Add the water chestnuts and continue to cook, stirring, for a few minutes. Add the shredded lettuce and cook for about 1 minute, or until the lettuce wilts. Add the garlic chives and cook for 15 seconds longer. Remove from the heat.

Spoon 3 to 4 tablespoons of the pork mixture into each lettuce cup and arrange on a platter or individual plates. Serve at once. This is delicious, but messy, finger food, so have napkins on hand.

squashes and gourds

Welcome to the family of cucurbits, which includes summer and winter squashes, melons, and gourds. They play a large role in Asian markets, and for the most part (excluding bitter melon) these fleshy vegetables are mild mannered in taste. You will find that they're not all that different in flavor from Western squashes such as zucchini, and they serve as a good foil for bolder ingredients in many dishes. As with most summer squashes, they are generally at their prime in warmer months. Kabocha, the only exception, is a winter squash.

squashes and gourds

bitter melon

ALSO KNOWN AS: *balsam pear, bitter cucumber, bitter gourd*

Whenever I'm rifling through the piles of bitter melon at my local market, I'm always shot a raised eyebrow or two: What's a white girl like her doing with a vegetable like that? It goes without saying that this wrinkly, green, cucumber-shaped melon is an acquired taste, even among Asians who appreciate bitter flavors. On the tongue it's shockingly bitter, but also delightfully cool because of the presence of quinine. From Southeast Asia to India, it has its devoted followers, and they're probably better off for it: bitter melon is said to purify the blood and boost the immune system. It is also sold in its baby stage, rock hard and extra-bumpy, sometimes still attached to its climbing vine, which is also eaten. It is rarely found outside of Asian markets.

bitter melon

SELECTING AND STORING: Bitter melons are warty by nature, but you should avoid any that are shriveled. Look for medium to small specimens that are plump and firm. Lighter green to yellowish melons are less bitter. Store them in loosely closed plastic bags in the refrigerator for up to a week.

HOW TO USE: Blanching and salting are the typical ways used to lessen the bitterness of this sharp-flavored vegetable, but some believe these efforts make little difference. Tiny bitter melons (which are often pickled in India) can be eaten seeds and all. Otherwise, the seeds should be scooped out with a spoon—no need to peel. Bitter melon is usually paired with bold flavors such as chili or fermented black beans. Thais bravely dip it raw into sauces pungent with shrimp paste, the Chinese often stuff it with seasoned ground pork, and the Indians stew it in curry.

bitter melon with egg

SERVES 4
as a side dish

No matter how good bitter melon is for you, you can't turn just everyone on to it. I made this dish for my husband and he looked at me in dismay after three bites. But eaten in small doses and accompanied by other dishes such as a coconut curry—and lots of rice—it can be an awakening for an otherwise jaded palate.

¾ pound bitter melons

4 eggs

1 tablespoon fish sauce

2 tablespoons canola oil

½ teaspoon sugar

½ cup fresh Thai basil leaves

Chili sauce such as *sambal oelek* for serving

Cut the bitter melons in half lengthwise, and use a spoon to scoop out the seeds. Slice the halves crosswise into ¼-inch-thick pieces. Set aside.

In a small bowl, whisk together the eggs and fish sauce until blended.

In a wok or large, deep skillet over medium-high heat, heat the oil. Add the bitter melons and stir-fry for about 3 minutes, or until they begin to soften. Immediately add the sugar to the egg mixture, then add the eggs to the pan. Toss to scramble with the bitter melons for another 1 minute or until the eggs have just set. Remove from the heat, add the basil, and toss to mix. Serve immediately with the chili sauce on the side.

bitter melon stuffed with pork and fermented black beans

SERVES 4
as a first course

In Chinatown delis and dim sum restaurants, a version of this classic dish is often one of the many offerings. Stuffing bitter melon with a savory filling (much like a stuffed bell pepper) and braising it until tender helps to counteract its bitter flavor. Accompany with steamed white rice.

2 bitter melons, about ½ pound each

½ pound lean ground pork

1 teaspoon finely chopped garlic

1 tablespoon finely chopped fresh ginger

¼ cup finely chopped red onion

½ cup chopped fresh cilantro

2 Thai chilies, finely chopped

½ teaspoon kosher salt

1 tablespoon fermented black beans, chopped

1 teaspoon sesame oil

1 cup chicken broth

Preheat the oven to 350°F.

Cut a slice off the top and bottom of each bitter melon. Cut the melons crosswise into 1-inch-thick slices (you should end up with at least 8 slices) and scoop out and discard the insides. Bring a saucepan filled with water to a boil, add the slices, and blanch for 2 minutes. Drain and immediately immerse in ice water to preserve the color. When cool, drain and place the slices, cut side up, in a baking pan just large enough to hold them all side by side and without touching.

In a bowl, combine the pork, garlic, ginger, onion, cilantro, chilies, salt, black beans, and sesame oil. Mix well to distribute all the ingredients evenly. Spoon a generous amount of pork mixture into each round. The pork should form a rounded top on the melon. In a small saucepan, bring the broth to a boil. Carefully pour the boiling broth over the stuffed slices. Cover the pan with aluminum foil or a lid.

Bake for 25 minutes, or until the filling is cooked through and the bitter melon is tender when pierced with a knife. Lift the stuffed bitter melon out of the broth and arrange on a platter. Serve at once.

bottle gourd

ALSO KNOWN AS: *calabash,* lauki, opo squash, po gwa *(Cantonese), white flowered gourd*

My first introduction to this versatile squash was at a little homespun Indian restaurant in San Francisco. The owner was especially proud of a deceptively rich curry, and for all his customers who couldn't believe the dish was vegetarian, he'd unveil the secret ingredient: bottle gourd, or what he called *lauki*. There are endless names for this popular vegetable, as it's grown throughout the world. Similar to fuzzy melon (page 78) in its mild summer squash flavor, bottle gourd has a meaty flesh that doesn't break down in long cooking. Its pale green, smooth skin is a constant, but the gourd comes in two forms. The one you'll often see in the markets tapers at the end like a bat, while the other is bottle shaped (it develops a woody shell when it matures that is used for making bottles and bowls). Bottle gourd is rarely found outside of Asian markets.

SELECTING AND STORING: Look for smaller gourds with smooth, unblemished skin. Store in the refrigerator in a loosely closed plastic bag for up to 2 weeks or sometimes longer; its tough skin extends its shelf life.

HOW TO USE: Peel the skin, cut in half lengthwise, and scoop out the seeds. Once cooked, bottle gourd turns slightly translucent. It makes a good neutral addition to full-flavored stir-fries, soups, and even rich dishes like curry.

bottle gourd

malaysian sweet-and-sour shrimp with bottle gourd

There's nothing meek or mild about this dish, spicy with ginger and chilies, sour with lime and tamarind, and tart-sweet with pineapple. The bottle gourd and shrimp soak up all the flavor. Fuzzy melon or chayote can be substituted for the squash. Serve with lots of rice to put out the fire.

SERVES 4

2 teaspoons finely chopped garlic

¼ cup peeled and finely chopped fresh ginger

1 to 2 serrano chilies, finely chopped

1 teaspoon freshly ground pepper

1 tablespoon canola oil

1 small bottle gourd, about ¾ pound, peeled, seeded, and chopped into ½-inch-thick pieces (about 2 ½ cups)

½ pound shrimp, peeled and deveined

1 tablespoon tamarind concentrate

2 tablespoons ketchup

½ teaspoon kosher salt

1 tomato, chopped (about ½ cup)

½ cup chopped fresh pineapple (¾-inch chunks)

2 tablespoons fresh lime juice

½ cup chopped fresh cilantro

In a small bowl, mix together the garlic, ginger, chilies, and pepper.

In a wok or large, deep skillet over medium-high heat, heat the oil. Add the garlic mixture and stir-fry for about 1 minute until fragrant. Add the bottle gourd and continue to stir-fry for another 7 to 10 minutes, or until the squash softens. Add the shrimp and cook for about 2 minutes, or until they begin to turn opaque. Add the tamarind, ketchup, and salt and mix well. Stir in the tomato, followed by the pineapple and then the lime juice. Cook for a few seconds more until the shrimp are opaque and the tomato has barely softened.

Remove from the heat, add the cilantro, and toss to mix. Transfer to a platter and serve at once.

indian-style whole fish stuffed with bottle gourd and tomato

If you haven't roasted a whole fish before, it's surprisingly simple. Not only is it a bargain (whole fish are always cheaper than fillets), but you can throw it in the oven, forget about it until it's done, and it makes a grand presentation. I like the meaty texture of bottle gourd, but fuzzy melon, chayote, or even zucchini would work fine in this recipe. The stuffing may be made up to a day ahead of time. Cook a pot of fragrant basmati rice as an accompaniment, and place an extra plate on the table for the bones.

SERVES 4

STUFFING:

2 tablespoons canola oil

1 teaspoon cumin seeds

2 teaspoons finely chopped garlic

2 teaspoons finely chopped fresh ginger

1 small serrano chili, finely chopped

1 small bottle gourd, about ¾ pound, peeled, seeded, and cut into ½-inch cubes (about 2 ½ cups)

2 ½ cups chopped tomato

¼ teaspoon sugar

1 teaspoon fresh lemon juice

½ teaspoon ground turmeric

2 teaspoons kosher salt

6 tablespoons chopped fresh cilantro

One 4-pound or two 2-pound whole fish such as striped bass, rock fish, or snapper, cleaned by your fishmonger

1 tablespoon kosher salt

1 tablespoon canola oil

4 lemon wedges

Preheat the oven to 400°F.

To make the stuffing, in a large sauté pan or skillet over medium-high heat, heat the oil. Add the cumin seeds and sauté for about 30 seconds, or until fragrant. Add the garlic, ginger, and chili and sauté for 30 seconds. Add the bottle gourd, tomato, sugar, lemon juice, turmeric, and salt and reduce the heat to medium-low. When the squash has just begun to get soft, after 10 to 12 minutes, remove from the heat and toss with the cilantro. Transfer to a bowl and let cool. (If working ahead of time, cover and store the stuffing in the refrigerator for up to 24 hours. Bring to room temperature before stuffing the fish.)

Meanwhile, prepare the fish: Rinse it, pat it dry with paper towels, and season the cavity and skin with the salt. Oil a roasting pan with the oil and place the fish in it. Fill the cavity with the stuffing, spooning any extra around the fish.

Bake for 20 to 30 minutes, or until the fish is opaque throughout when pierced with a knife. Serve pieces of fish with the stuffing and a wedge of lemon.

chayote

ALSO KNOWN AS: *christophene, mirliton, vegetable pear*

A pale shade of green and shaped like a pear, chayote is native to Mexico and Central America, but it has been embraced by Asians (as well as Southerners who call it mirliton). Beneath its thin skin is crisp, white flesh not unlike that of an apple, with a refreshing mild taste that is reminiscent of a cucumber. Although I enjoy chayote raw, it has a slightly slippery quality when it's first peeled, and most recipes call for it to be cooked. Like many of the squashes in the Asian kitchen, chayote is a blank slate, perfect for pairing with just about anything.

chayote

SELECTING AND STORING: Select unblemished chayote with smooth, unwrinkled skin. Store in a loosely-sealed plastic bag in the refrigerator for up to a month.

HOW TO USE: Chayote must be peeled and, if desired, the soft, single edible seed removed (I take it out). It's interchangeable with most summer squashes such as zucchini, as well as many of the other Asian gourds, such as fuzzy melon and bottle gourd. Try shredding it and adding it to a *raita*, or slicing it thinly and floating it in a soup (it will become beautifully translucent).

chilled avocado-chayote soup

Chayote crosses many borders. I came up with this decadent soup when I was on vacation in Baja and had access to an abundance of dirt-cheap avocados and chayotes. Using water instead of chicken stock makes it vegan, but it's so rich that no one will believe it when you tell them. Try to find Hass avocados for their silky texture and big flavor, and although I prefer to chill the soup, you might find that you like it hot, which gives it a lighter taste. Try serving it in little espresso cups as a teaser before a meal.

SERVES 4 TO 6
as a first course

2 tablespoons canola oil

½ cup chopped yellow onion

3 small chayotes, about 1½ pounds total, peeled, seeded, and chopped

2 ½ cups chicken broth or water

4 ripe avocados

¼ cup fresh lime juice

2 Thai chilies or 1 serrano chili, thinly sliced (optional)

1 tablespoon kosher salt

1 teaspoon sugar

Chopped fresh cilantro for garnish

In a large saucepan over medium heat, heat the oil and sauté the onion for 3 to 5 minutes, or until translucent. Add the chayotes and the chicken broth or water and bring to a boil. Reduce the heat to a simmer and cook for 15 to 20 minutes, or until the chayote is tender.

Meanwhile, pit, peel, and cube the avocados, removing any brown spots. Place in a bowl and sprinkle a bit of the lime juice on them, to prevent browning. Set aside.

Remove the pan from the heat and pour the contents into a blender and puree. (Depending on the size of your blender, it might be necessary to do this in batches.) Return half of the puree to the pan, pouring it through a strainer if there are any lumps.

Add three-fourths of the avocado cubes, the remaining lime juice, the chilies, the salt, and the sugar to the blender. Puree until smooth and then pour it through a strainer to remove any remaining lumps. Return it to the pan with the rest of the puree and stir to combine. Transfer to a clean container, cover, and refrigerate until chilled. Cover and chill the remaining avocado cubes.

To serve, ladle into chilled bowls. Garnish with the avocado cubes and the cilantro.

節
瓜

fuzzy melon

ALSO KNOWN AS: mo gwa *(Cantonese), hairy cucumber, hairy melon*

In its edible, and immature, stage, this mild gourd looks like it has a five o'clock shadow. But as it ages, it gradually loses its fuzzy covering. Similar to bottle gourd in many ways, fuzzy melon is distinct because of its lightly mottled, darker green skin. It comes in two forms: one is bat shaped, while the other is squat and oblong. If you have a household that refuses even a bite of squishy zucchini, try fuzzy melon (or bottle gourd, page 72) on them. You'll be surprised to see them cleaning their plates. Fuzzy melon is rarely found outside of Asian markets.

fuzzy melon

SELECTING AND STORING: Look for younger, smaller gourds with unblemished, still fuzzy skin. Store in the refrigerator in a loosely closed plastic bag for up to a week or more.

HOW TO USE: If you find fuzzy melon at its hairy stage (which should also be its sweetest), remove the hair by gently rubbing it off, then halve lengthwise, and scoop out the seeds. Peeling the skin is optional. Like any summer squash, fuzzy melon can be used in a multitude of dishes, from soups to stir-fries. It also is delicious stuffed with ground pork following the method for the bitter melon recipe on page 71.

sesame noodles with fuzzy melon and ground beef

Sesame seeds are one of the cornerstones of Korean cooking, and this quick and homey recipe has them times three: ground, whole, and as sesame oil. You can use any-sized egg noodles you please, but I like the flat, fettuccine-sized ones best for this recipe. Get more sesame flavor from toasted sesame seeds by toasting them even more in a dry skillet for about a minute until they are aromatic, taking care not to burn them. To make the ground sesame seeds, place toasted sesame seeds in a spice grinder or clean coffee grinder and quickly (like a nanosecond) grind to a rough powder.

SERVES 4

2 tablespoons canola oil

4 teaspoons finely chopped garlic

3 tablespoons finely chopped shallot

1 pound lean ground beef

1 teaspoon kosher salt

1 fuzzy melon, about ¾ pound, peeled, halved lengthwise, seeded, and cut into ½-inch-thick pieces

2 tablespoons ground toasted sesame seeds (see recipe introduction)

1 tablespoon chili sauce, such as *sambal oelek*

2 tablespoons soy sauce

¾ pound fresh Asian egg noodles

2 teaspoons sesame oil

2 teaspoons sesame seeds

4 green onions, white and green parts, sliced thinly

In a wok or large, deep skillet over high heat, heat the oil. Add the garlic and shallot and stir-fry for 30 seconds. Add the ground beef and salt and stir-fry, breaking up the meat, for 3 to 5 minutes, or until starting to brown. Reduce the heat to medium and add the fuzzy melon, ground sesame seeds, chili sauce, and soy sauce. Cook, stirring occasionally, for 10 to 12 minutes, or until the melon is soft and translucent.

Meanwhile, bring a large pot filled with water to a boil. Add the noodles and cook for 3 to 5 minutes, or until just tender. The timing will depend on the kind of noodles you choose. Drain the noodles and toss with the sesame oil. Transfer to a platter.

Spoon the fuzzy melon and beef mixture over the noodles. Garnish with the sesame seeds and green onions and serve.

fuzzy melon and fresh corn with yogurt

SERVES 4

When summer rolls around and fresh corn is in the market, grab a couple ears for this quick Indian-inspired dish. The fuzzy melon turns a stunning bright yellow with the addition of turmeric. To get extra corn flavor, draw the blunt side of a knife down the length of the cob and use all of the milky liquid that is expressed.

2 tablespoons canola oil

1 teaspoon cumin seeds

1 tablespoon peeled finely chopped fresh ginger

2 teaspoons finely chopped garlic

1 fuzzy melon, about 1 pound, peeled, halved lengthwise, seeded, and cut into ½-inch pieces (about 3 cups)

Kernels from 2 ears of corn (about 1 cup)

1 serrano chili, chopped (optional)

1 tablespoon ground coriander

½ teaspoon ground turmeric

1 teaspoon kosher salt

½ cup plain yogurt

½ cup chopped fresh cilantro

In a wok or deep skillet over medium-high heat, heat the oil. Add the cumin seeds. When they become aromatic, after about 30 seconds, add the ginger and garlic and cook for 30 more seconds. Add the fuzzy melon, corn, chili, coriander, turmeric, and salt and mix well. Add the yogurt and stir to combine. Reduce the heat to low, cover, and cook for 15 minutes, or until the fuzzy melon is tender and translucent.

Transfer to a bowl, stir in the cilantro, and serve.

kabocha squash

At my local supermarket, I can now find kabocha alongside the other winter squashes such as acorn and butternut. This squat, round gourd with mottled green skin is similar in size to the small sugar pumpkins used for baking. Its bright orange flesh is sweet enough for desserts (such as in a Thai coconut custard) but mild enough to swab with miso and put on the grill, Japanese style.

kabocha squash

SELECTING AND STORING: Select a kabocha that feels heavy for its size. I always buy the smallest one I can find, usually 2 or 3 pounds, or end up having far more than I can use at once. Store in a cool, dry place for up to a month or more. Cut pieces of squash may be kept in an airtight container in the refrigerator for up to 2 days.

HOW TO USE: From roasting to stewing, kabocha can be cooked just like any winter squash. To cube it, you must remove the skin, taking care to keep track of all your fingers in the process (see the curry recipe following). Kabocha squash pairs naturally with anything coconut, from curries to sweet custards. The Japanese slice it thinly and fry it for tempura. And like all my favorite winter squashes, I love it roasted with a generous pat of butter, salt, pepper, and a squeeze of lime. To roast the squash whole, slice it in half and place it flesh side down in a roasting pan in a 400°F oven until tender when pierced with a knife.

thai red curry with kabocha squash and shrimp

You may not have come across this Thai curry before, but coconut and kabocha are a classic combination. I prefer to add shrimp, but a traditional addition is roasted duck. The key to making a good curry is to fry the curry paste in coconut cream. It brings out a deep, mellow flavor, reducing any potential bitterness. To secure the coconut cream, do not shake the can of coconut milk before you open it (you will probably need to open two cans for this recipe, as most hold less than the 2 ½ cups needed). Remove the lid and skim off the layer of cream sitting on top of the milk to use for frying. Gauge how much curry paste to use by tasting your particular brand, as each one varies in heat and saltiness. If kabocha squash isn't available, butternut squash makes a good substitute.

SERVES 4 TO 6 *Serve the curry with lots of jasmine rice.*

1 small kabocha squash, about 2 pounds

2 ½ cups coconut milk (see recipe introduction)

1 to 2 tablespoons Thai red curry paste

1 ½ teaspoons sugar

3 tablespoons fish sauce

½ cup chicken broth

2 lemongrass stalks, bottom 4 inches only, tough outer leaves removed, halved crosswise, and bruised

½ pound large shrimp, peeled and deveined

½ cup fresh or frozen peas

4 Roma (plum) tomatoes, quartered lengthwise

Using a sturdy chef's knife or cleaver, split the kabocha squash into quarters through the stem end. Remove the seeds and fibrous strands with a spoon. Place the squash on a cut side to steady it, then carefully, aiming your knife downward, remove the skin. Cut enough 1-inch chunks to make 4 cups.

To make the curry, heat a wok over high heat. Scoop the thick coconut cream off the top of the coconut milk and add it to the pan, followed by the red curry paste. Fry the paste in the cream, stirring constantly, for about 3 minutes, or until it becomes aromatic and richer in color. Add the sugar and fish sauce and stir to combine. Pour in the remaining coconut milk and the broth, mix well, reduce the heat to low, and add the lemongrass and squash. Cook for 20 to 30 minutes, or until the squash is tender when pierced with a fork.

Add the shrimp and peas and cook for 3 to 5 minutes, or until the shrimp are opaque. Add the tomatoes and cook for 1 minute longer until heated through. Turn into a bowl and serve at once.

絲
瓜

luffa squash

ALSO KNOWN AS: *Chinese okra, silk squash,* sing qua *(Cantonese), sponge gourd*

As pleasant as most summer squash is for eating, it is usually a backdrop for the other flavors. But luffa squash is much spongier than most gourds, and when quickly stir-fried, it has a fantastic silky texture and subtle sweet taste that's lovely on its own. With its dark green, rather tough skin and thin, ridged, slightly curving body that grows up to a foot long, the luffa is impossible to miss in the market. A smooth variety is also eaten (and in its mature stage is dried to use as a scrub for the bath, hence the name), although I seldom see it in the markets.

luffa squash

SELECTING AND STORING: Look for luffa squashes that are relatively small and are firm and unshriveled (make sure the growing end is not soft). Store in a loosely closed plastic bag in the refrigerator for up to a week.

HOW TO USE: Although some sources will tell you that the youngest luffas don't need to be peeled, I think they do. The skin is usually very bitter and should be removed completely, so that you're left only with the pale green flesh. There's no need to seed a luffa; in fact, luffas can be eaten raw. Literally a sponge, it will soak up whatever flavors with which you pair it. It's used in coconut curries and brothy soups and pairs nicely with shrimp and squid. The cooking time is remarkably short.

stir-fried luffa squash with diced shrimp and garlic

I can't tell you how much I love this simple, ten-minute dish. Like many Asian recipes, the meat—in this case, shrimp—is the flavoring, and the vegetable is the focal point. Luffa squash is seasoned simply to show off its supple texture and slightly sweet flavor. When Kasma Loha-unchit, who gave me this recipe, cooks it, she cuts the luffa into chunks bigger than you'd expect would cook in time, but they cook quickly, so the size works perfectly.

SERVES 4

2 tablespoons canola oil

4 cloves garlic, chopped

10 shrimp, peeled, deveined, and finely chopped

4 luffa squashes, about 1 ½ pounds total, peeled and cut into 1 ½-inch chunks on the diagonal

1 tablespoon fish sauce, or to taste

White pepper to taste

In a wok or large, deep skillet over medium-high heat, heat the oil. Add the garlic and stir-fry for 15 seconds until fragrant. Add the shrimp and stir-fry for 1 to 2 minutes, or until the shrimp begin to turn opaque. Add the squashes and stir-fry for a minute or so until the squashes begin to cook and turn just a little translucent. Add the fish sauce and pepper, stir well, and serve at once.

Bruce Hill's luffa squash, tomato, and mint salad

SERVES 4
as a side dish

Typical of Bruce's cooking, this summer salad lets the squash speak for itself. White balsamic vinegar is available at some specialty food stores.

2 tablespoons white balsamic vinegar

¼ cup canola oil

Kosher salt and freshly ground pepper to taste

2 cups peeled and sliced luffa squash

2 cups stemmed and halved cherry tomatoes

3 tablespoons finely shredded fresh mint leaves

In a small bowl, whisk together the vinegar, oil, salt, and pepper.

Place the squash slices and cherry tomatoes in a bowl and pour in the dressing. Toss well. Just before serving, toss with the mint.

Bruce Hill on **luffa squash**

I first met chef Bruce Hill at San Francisco's Alemany Farmers' Market, a mecca for impeccable Asian vegetables. Small-plot farmers hawk everything from bitter melon greens to daikon tops and fenugreek leaves—things that you rarely see elsewhere. Bruce, who turned me on to luffa squash, has a signature style of cooking that fuses East with West with exceptional intelligence and restraint. "I think the texture of this squash is really great," Bruce says. "I like the mouthful. The sweetness lends itself to things like tomatoes as well as raw cremini mushrooms." He suggests serving it stir-fried with corn, shrimp, *shiso* leaves, and a dash of Shaoxing wine. Bruce looks for luffa that are no more than a couple inches in diameter and avoids any that have a hollow feel and big seeds inside.

winter melon

冬瓜

ALSO KNOWN AS: *ash gourd, preserving melon, wax gourd, winter squash*

Winter melon would make a good stand-in for the Great Pumpkin. Actually a summer squash, it gets massive (up to 100 pounds) and has green skin sometimes brushed with orange and unevenly covered with what looks like a light coating of frost. You'll rarely see it whole in the market. Instead, it's generally sold in big, fleshy white slices containing seeds and wrapped in plastic. The mild, juicy flesh is full of water and turns almost completely translucent when cooked. For Chinese banquets, a winter melon soup is often served in a tureen made from a decoratively carved winter melon itself. You'll seldom see winter melon outside of Asian markets.

winter melon

SELECTING AND STORING: Look for firm, white flesh and a neutral smell. Cut winter melon can be stored for a day or two in the refrigerator, while a whole melon will keep for up to a year in a (large) cool, dark space.

HOW TO USE: Peel away the skin and scoop out and discard the seeds. Cut the flesh into chunks or slices to use in soups or stews. I've eaten winter melon in a red Thai curry with salmon and its succulent flesh contrasted beautifully with the rich fish. The Chinese pickle and candy it, too, but their most traditional use of this giant vegetable is in a delicate brothy soup with ham.

Chris Yeo's winter melon soup with meatballs and crab claws

This soup is one of my favorite recipes in Chris's repertory. It's delicious, beautiful, and surprisingly easy to prepare. Don't skip the fried garlic. It really makes the dish. For a more interesting presentation, try slicing the winter melon in long, thin slices.

SERVES 4 TO 6

1 pound lean ground pork

½ teaspoon kosher salt

½ teaspoon freshly ground pepper

1 teaspoon cornstarch

¾ cup canola oil

¼ cup chopped garlic

2 ½ quarts chicken broth

5 tablespoons fish sauce

2 teaspoons sugar

1 lemongrass stalk, bottom 4 inches only, tough outer leaves removed, halved crosswise, and bruised

1-pound piece winter melon, peeled, seeded, and cut into ½-inch-thick slices

6 crab claws

Chopped fresh cilantro for garnish

In a bowl, season the ground pork with the salt and pepper. Sprinkle with the cornstarch and combine well. To make the meatballs, gently roll the pork between your palms into balls 1 inch in diameter. Wet your hands with water as necessary to keep them from sticking to the pork. Set the meatballs aside.

In a small saucepan over medium-high heat, heat the oil. Add the garlic and fry for about 2 minutes, or until golden brown. Using a mesh skimmer, transfer the garlic to paper towels to drain. Set aside.

In a large pot, bring the chicken broth to a boil over high heat. Reduce the heat so the broth is at a gentle simmer and add the fish sauce, sugar, lemongrass, and winter melon. Cook for about 5 minutes, or until the winter melon is translucent. Add the meatballs and crab claws. Simmer for 10 to 12 minutes, or until the meatballs and crab claws are cooked through. (Turn the meatballs if necessary for even cooking.)

Skim off any fat from the surface of the broth. Ladle the soup into bowls and garnish with the fried garlic and cilantro. Set out the crab crackers and serve immediately.

Chris Yeo on **winter melon**

Singapore is one of the best one-stop spots for great Asian food. Like the United States, it's an immigrant country and its cuisine is a mixed bag. You can find everything from Chinese, Malay, and Indonesian to Indian and Nonya cooking in a single food court. Singaporean-born Chris Yeo opened Straits Café in San Francisco, and his Nonya (also known as Straits Chinese) cooking, a hybrid of Chinese and Malay, proved such a success that he opened a second location south of the city. Chris's mother used to make a variation of this soup for him, and it's also typically included on the menu in a classic Nonya restaurant. "Winter melon doesn't have any flavor really," Chris says. "It goes best with a clear soup, so that it's not overpowered."

four

beans and things

This is the grab bag. Reach in and you will find familiar friends like eggplant and mushrooms. But in the Asian market even these commoners come in new shapes and sizes, from little green-and-white Thai eggplants to tall and willowy enoki mushrooms. And then there are some of my personal favorites, including green papaya (technically a fruit, but used like a vegetable), loopy long beans, and soybeans that are eaten straight from their pods. Many of these nutritious vegetables span cultures—even beyond Asia—and some, like snow peas, you'll easily find in your local supermarket.

beans and things

eggplant

矮
瓜

If you only shopped in mainstream American markets, it would be easy to think that this versatile vegetable stops with the purple globe variety. Asians, on the other hand, expect to find eggplants in many shapes and sizes. Native to India, and ranging in color from green to white to purple, there are far too many eggplant varieties to name them all. Chinese and Japanese eggplants are the most common here. Although both are long and slim, Chinese eggplant has pale lavender skin and a creamier texture when cooked than its dark purple Japanese cousin. In Southeast Asian markets I can find the hard, golf-ball-sized, green-and-white-streaked Thai eggplants typically used in curries. The Thais also love bitter pea eggplants, which grow in clusters and are eaten raw, usually dipped into a sauce called *nam prik,* or cooked and mellowed in curries.

eggplant (Chinese, Japanese, Thai)

SELECTING AND STORING: No matter what kind of variety you're choosing, look for taut, smooth skin without dimples, cuts, or bruises. Store in a loosely closed plastic bag in the refrigerator. The shelf life depends on the type of eggplant, but most will keep for up to a week or longer.

HOW TO USE: Many Western recipes call for salting globe eggplants first, to draw out their bitter juices, but I don't find this step necessary for any variety. And unless there's a specific reason to remove the skin (such as when you're mashing the cooked flesh), eggplant is generally prepared with the skin on. Eggplant is wonderful grilled because it picks up the smoky flavor, and the small Thai ones fare well in long-cooked curries and stews.

fiery grilled eggplant and chili salad

SERVES 4
as a side dish

The first time I tried a version of this Thai dish, prepared by Kasma Loha-unchit, my lips were on fire, but I couldn't stop eating it. If your hands are at all sensitive to chilies, take my advice and don some gloves. Kasma includes cooked shrimp in her salad as well, but I find it's just as satisfying without it. I like Chinese eggplant because of its slippery softness, but Japanese eggplant is a fine substitute.

DRESSING:

3 to 5 Thai chilies, finely chopped

¼ cup fresh lime juice

3 tablespoons fish sauce

2 teaspoons sugar

4 long Chinese eggplants, tops removed

4 jalapeño chilies, preferably a mix of green and red

1 shallot, thinly sliced in half-moons

1 hard-boiled egg, peeled and cut into 6 wedges

Small handful of fresh cilantro leaves

Prepare a charcoal grill. While the coals are getting hot, make the dressing: In a small bowl, stir together the Thai chilies, lime juice, fish sauce, and sugar until the sugar dissolves. Set aside.

When the fire is very hot, place the whole eggplants and jalapeños on the grill. Turn both frequently until they are charred, softened, and cooked through, about 15 minutes. Remove the eggplants and chilies from the grill and place them in a paper bag, close it tightly, and allow them to steam. When cool enough to handle, peel off the charred skin from the eggplants and the chilies (using gloves if necessary for the chilies).

Cut each eggplant in half lengthwise, and cut each half lengthwise into quarters. Cut the quarters crosswise into bite-sized pieces each about 1 ½ inches long. Remove the stems and seeds from the chilies, and slice them lengthwise into narrow strips.

Arrange the eggplant pieces on a platter, and scatter the chilies and the shallot slices on top. Pour the dressing over the salad. Garnish with the egg wedges and cilantro leaves. Serve at room temperature.

chicken coconut curry with eggplant and green beans

SERVES 4 TO 6

In Asia, just like anywhere, the cuisines of neighboring countries have been fused, mixed, and matched. This homey dish, which uses the coconut milk and lemongrass typical of Thai curries and the coriander and cumin of India, is a good example of that tradition. I like to grind whole spices fresh in a clean coffee grinder. But if you're in a rush, you can replace the coriander, turmeric, and cumin with 1 ½ tablespoons good-quality curry powder. I use dark chicken meat in this dish because it's more flavorful and moist than breast meat. The curry is even better the next day. Serve it with rice or Vietnamese style, with crusty French bread for dipping.

3 tablespoons canola oil

1 tablespoon finely chopped fresh ginger

2 teaspoons finely chopped garlic

2 lemongrass stalks, bottom 4 inches only, tough outer leaves removed, and finely chopped

1 shallot, finely chopped

2 Thai chilies or 1 serrano chili, finely chopped

1 ½ pounds boneless, skinless chicken thighs cut into 1-inch pieces

½ teaspoon kosher salt

2 teaspoons ground coriander

1 teaspoon turmeric

1 teaspoon ground cumin

1 cup coconut milk

1 cup chicken broth

¼ pound green beans, trimmed and cut crosswise into 1-inch pieces

6 Thai eggplants, tops removed and quartered lengthwise, or 2 Japanese eggplants, tops removed, quartered lengthwise, and sliced crosswise into 1-inch pieces

2 tablespoons fish sauce

1 teaspoon sugar

3 tablespoons tamarind concentrate

In a large pot over medium heat, heat the oil. Add the ginger, garlic, lemongrass, shallot, and chilies and cook for 1 to 2 minutes, or until fragrant. Add the chicken, sprinkling it with salt, and cook for about 5 minutes, or until the chicken is opaque.

Add the coriander, turmeric, and cumin and stir to coat the chicken. Pour in the coconut milk and chicken broth, bring to a simmer, and then add the green beans and eggplants. Reduce the heat to low, cover, and cook for about 30 minutes, or until the chicken is tender.

Add the fish sauce, sugar, and tamarind gradually, tasting to make sure there is a good balance between tart, sweet, and salty. Continue to cook for another 5 minutes to marry the flavors, then transfer to a bowl and serve.

Sukhi Singh's bharta

SERVES 6 TO 8
as an appetizer
or side dish

Traditionally, this northern Indian preparation—almost a silky puree—is served as a kind of side dish and is scooped up with chapati to eat. But it's also good served with slices of French bread, pita bread, or crackers as an appetizer. Although Sukhi calls for broiling the eggplant, it also can be grilled over hot coals. Don't be afraid to char the eggplant completely black. Once you peel it, you'll have a delicious smoky flavor. Bharta keeps well and can be made a day ahead of time.

6 Japanese eggplants or 1 globe eggplant, about
   1½ pounds total

½ cup canola oil

2 teaspoons grated fresh ginger

1 large red onion, finely chopped
   (about 1½ cups)

2 large tomatoes, chopped (about 2 cups)

½ teaspoon freshly ground pepper

1½ teaspoons garam masala

1 tablespoon salt

½ cup chopped fresh cilantro

Preheat the broiler. Place the whole eggplant(s) on a baking sheet and slide it under a broiler about 1 inch from the heat. Broil, turning to char evenly, for 20 to 30 minutes. The eggplant(s) should be completely black, soft, and wrinkled. Remove from the broiler and set aside to cool.

Trim and peel the cooled eggplant(s), but don't worry if you can't get all the charred skin off (it actually adds a little more flavor). Cut into pieces against the grain. Try to conserve as much liquid as possible, as the flavor is in the juice. Place in a bowl and mash with a fork.

In a large, heavy-bottomed skillet over medium heat, heat the oil. Add the ginger and sauté for 30 seconds until fragrant. Add the onion and cook for 5 minutes, or until translucent. Add the tomatoes and cook for 2 minutes, or until beginning to soften. Stir in the pepper, garam masala, and salt and add the eggplant. Reduce the heat to low and cook for 15 minutes, stirring occasionally, until all the flavors have melded together and the *bharta* is relatively smooth.

Transfer to a bowl and garnish with the cilantro. Serve hot or at room temperature.

Sukhi Singh on **eggplant**

If you're trying to find Sukhi Singh's booth at one of the many Bay Area farmers' markets, just look for a crowd four or five people deep. While Sukhi hands out samples of her prepared products, which are sold under the label Sukhi's Quick-n-Ezee Indian Foods, everyone leans in to get a samosa or elbows their way to a taste of one of her fantastic chutneys or curry pastes.

One of her most popular items is her *bharta,* a traditional Punjabi dish made from roasted eggplants. "Eggplant is one of the staples of Indian cooking," Sukhi says. With its mild flavor and creamy texture, it's perfect for soaking up the plethora of spices Indian cooks regularly use. When purchasing eggplants, Sukhi looks for crisp specimens, with smooth and shiny skin. "We go through twenty-five cases of eggplants a week," Sukhi says. "And the longer you cook eggplant, the tastier it gets."

green papaya

Although it's technically an unripe fruit, I've included green papaya in this book because, like green mangoes, it's treated as a vegetable in cooking (plus, life shouldn't be lived without a taste of Vietnamese or Thai green papaya salad). On the outside, green papaya is shaped similarly to the variety of papaya we eat ripe. The difference is that it's rock hard and green and the flesh and seeds are snowy white. Unripe papaya has a mild, vaguely sour taste, and I liken its texture to celery root—crunchy but not crisp. You're not as likely to find it in Chinese markets, as it's predominately used in Southeast Asian cooking.

green papaya

SELECTING AND STORING: Green papaya should have no trace of yellow or orange, no bruises, and should be firm and heavy in your hand. Store it in a cool, dry place or in a loosely closed plastic bag in the refrigerator for up to a week or more.

HOW TO USE: Always peel, halve, and seed green papaya before using for a recipe. Then, most often, it's shredded and made into a salad, although it's also used in savory pancakes and as a tenderizer for Indian lamb kabobs.

Mai Pham's green papaya salad

SERVES 4
as a side dish

This salad is often made with a generous amount of chili and lime, along with dried shrimp and, in some instances, with pickled crab. This version is much tamer but just as mouthwatering. Palm sugar, made from the sap of various varieties of palm tree, is sold in tubs and blocks in Asian markets.

1 small green papaya

2 cloves garlic

3 Thai chilies, chopped

1 tablespoon dried shrimp, soaked in hot water for 15 minutes and drained

1 tablespoon palm sugar or light brown sugar

2 tablespoons fish sauce

3 tablespoons fresh lime juice

¼ cup cut-up (2-inch pieces) raw long beans or green beans (optional)

5 cherry tomatoes, stemmed and halved

⅓ cup chopped unsalted roasted peanuts

¼ head green cabbage, cut into thin wedges and leaves separated

Peel the papaya and cut in half lengthwise. Scoop out the seeds and discard. With a Japanese mandoline or with a box grater, cut the papaya into thin, long strands about 1/16 inch wide. Set aside.

Place the garlic and chilies in a large mortar and pound until they're broken down. Add the dried shrimp and pound slightly. Add the sugar and fish sauce, then pound a few more times to allow the seasonings and juices to blend together. Mix in the lime juice and transfer to a bowl.

Add the papaya to the mortar (in batches if necessary). Using a spoon to turn the papaya lightly pound it so that it barely bruises. Add the green beans, if using, and tomatoes. Pound lightly, and stir in half of the peanuts. Transfer to the bowl and toss all the ingredients together. Transfer the salad to a serving plate lined with the cabbage leaves. Garnish with the remaining peanuts.

Mai Pham on **green papaya**

In Thailand, where Mai Pham, the author of *The Best of Vietnamese and Thai Cooking*, spent much of her life, you can't go too far without running into a street vendor hawking *som tum*, or green papaya salad. "It's part of everyday life there," Mai recounts. "Sometimes you can just pick green papayas from the trees that grow alongside the road." Now a resident of Sacramento, California, where she owns the celebrated Lemon Grass restaurant, Mai has resorted to Asian markets for her supply. She looks for smooth-skinned fruits that are heavy in the hand. Green papaya salad is traditionally lightly pounded with a wooden mortar and pestle, so that it's just slightly bruised.

long beans

豆角

ALSO KNOWN AS: *asparagus bean, snake bean, yard-long bean*

There's something magical about long beans. They look like a vegetable out of a Dr. Seuss book. Growing up to three feet in length, they are sold in Asian—and sometimes Western—markets, bound with a rubber band or tied in one big knot. Two types of long beans are available, light green and dark green, but many consider the latter to be the tastier. Don't try to compare them to green beans. Much heartier, they are actually related to black-eyed peas and taste nutty rather than sweet. Long beans are used in many different cuisines, from Thai to Indian to Chinese.

long beans

SELECTING AND STORING: Long beans are floppy by nature. The best indicator of freshness is an absence of black spots and shriveling. Long beans can be stored in a loosely closed plastic bag in the refrigerator for up to a week, but they taste best when used as soon as possible.

HOW TO USE: Because long beans are rather fibrous, I find them best chopped into crunchy pieces no more than a couple inches long. Some recipes call for them to be cut even smaller. Because of their sturdy nature, long beans hold up well in stir-fries and stews. I love them with bold flavors such as peanut sauce, bean paste, or chili sauce. They're also delicious stir-fried with shrimp and loads of Thai basil.

long beans with dried shrimp

I'm a big fan of the pungent fish sauces and shrimp pastes critical to much of Southeast Asian cooking, but not everyone savors such strong flavors. To tone down the shrimp flavor of this Malaysian dish, halve the amount of dried shrimp and replace it with an extra tablespoon of chopped garlic. Traditionally, the paste used in this recipe would most likely be pounded in a mortar, but a blender will quickly get the results you need.

SERVES 4 TO 6
as a side dish

2 tablespoons dried shrimp

1 cup hot water

½ cup chopped shallot

1 Thai chili, coarsely chopped

5 teaspoons chopped garlic

½ pound long beans, trimmed and cut into
   1-inch pieces (about 2 cups)

2 tablespoons canola oil

½ teaspoon fresh ground pepper

1 teaspoon kosher salt

3 tablespoons fresh lime juice

In a bowl, soak the shrimp in the hot water for 15 minutes. Drain the shrimp, reserving the water. In a blender, combine the rehydrated shrimp, the shallot, chili, and garlic and blend. If the paste is too dry to blend efficiently, add a little of the shrimp water. Use a rubber spatula to help push the ingredients down toward the blade (but don't do this with the blender running). Blend until as smooth as possible. A few lumps are fine.

Bring a large pot filled with water to a boil and blanch the long beans for 2 minutes. Drain and rinse with cold water.

In a wok or large, deep skillet over high heat, heat the oil. Add the shrimp paste and stir-fry for 1 to 2 minutes until fragrant. Add the long beans, stir-fry to mix thoroughly, and reduce the heat. Add 2 tablespoons of the reserved water, the pepper, salt, and lime juice. Cook over low heat for 2 minutes to marry the flavors. Drain off any liquid before transferring to a serving dish. Serve at once.

Naomi and Jeffrey's long beans with coconut and mustard seeds

Following is my version of a south Indian long bean recipe that appears in Naomi and Jeffrey's comprehensive cookbook, Seductions of Rice. *Unlike the rich northern Indian cooking that is prevalent in restaurants in the United States, southern cooking tends to be lighter and uses coconut and fresh curry leaves.*

SERVES 4 TO 6

½ cup unsweetened fresh, frozen, or dried grated
   coconut
½ cup plus 1 tablespoon minced shallot
¼ teaspoon freshly ground pepper
¼ teaspoon cayenne pepper
½ teaspoon ground cumin
¼ teaspoon ground turmeric
1 tablespoon vegetable oil
1 dried red chili
½ teaspoon brown mustard seeds
1 fresh curry leaf (optional)
1 pound long beans, trimmed and cut into
   ¼-inch pieces (about 4 cups)
1 cup hot water
2 teaspoons salt

In a food processor, combine the coconut, the ½ cup shallot, the black pepper, the cayenne pepper, and the cumin and process until a dry paste, or *masala* (blended spice mixture), forms. Turn out into a bowl, stir in the turmeric, and set aside.

In a large wok or deep, heavy pot over medium-high heat, heat the oil. Toss in the chili and mustard seeds, stir, and then add the curry leaf and cook, for about 30 seconds, or until the mustard seeds pop. Lower the heat slightly and add the 1 tablespoon shallot.

Add the *masala* and stir-fry for 3 minutes, or until golden brown and aromatic. Add the long beans and turn and stir for several minutes, mixing well. Add the hot water and salt, bring to a boil, cover, and cook for 3 minutes. Stir again, reduce the heat to medium, cover, and let the beans continue to cook for 10 to 15 minutes, or until they are tender but still firm.

Uncover and cook for another 1 to 2 minutes, to evaporate any remaining water, then turn onto a plate and serve.

Naomi Duguid and Jeffrey Alford on **long beans**

Naomi Duguid and Jeffrey Alford have traveled all over the world—but particularly to Asia—photographing people and documenting their recipes in a number of intelligent cookbooks, including *Flatbreads and Flavors*, *Seductions of Rice*, and *Hot Sour Salty Sweet: A Culinary Journey Through Southeast Asia*. But even in Toronto, where they live, wonderful Asian markets abound. "When we come home from a trip, we're still away in some ways," says Naomi. "Toronto is an extraordinary place to shop. But by the time long beans get to the market, unless they're locally grown, they can be a little peaked. I toss them into a pot of boiling water for a second—it takes away the 'I've traveled a long way' look." Naomi finds long beans more versatile than green beans because they can stand rougher handling.

mushrooms shiitake, enoki, oyster, tree ear

These fresh Asian mushrooms are now available at many gourmet markets. They are also available fresh in Chinatown markets, but you'll find that shiitake and tree ear in particular are preferred dried by most Chinese cooks.

Shiitake are also commonly known as Chinese black mushrooms and have brown caps and creamy-colored gills. Dried shiitakes are sold in bulk in Chinese apothecaries, as they are believed to do everything from bolster the immune system to fight cancer. Oyster mushrooms are shaped like a fan. They smell vaguely of the sea, range from white to pale gray. White enoki are the ballerina of mushrooms, with spaghetti-skinny stems, tiny caps, and a delicate taste to match. They are often sold vacuum packed. Fleshy and brown tree ear (also called cloud ear and black fungus) mushrooms are the hardest to come by fresh, although they're readily available dried in Asian markets.

mushrooms, clockwise from bottom left: tree ear, enoki, shiitake, oyster

SELECTING AND STORING: Look for fresh mushrooms that are plump and moist, with no sign of slime. Store them in a brown paper bag in the bottom of the refrigerator.

HOW TO USE: Shiitakes are hearty enough to act as a meat substitute. The large fresh caps are good grilled. Remove any tough stems before using. Oyster mushrooms rarely need to be trimmed, but they reduce in size quite a bit when cooked. I like them best in a quick stir-fry and find that they get too waterlogged in soup. Enoki mushrooms come with the matted roots attached. Simply cut this off, separate the mushrooms, and try tossing them raw in a salad. Tree ear are delicious slivered and cooked in traditional Chinese hot-and-sour soup or in a stir-fry that needs some good crunchy texture.

five-spice chicken stew with shiitake mushrooms

This hearty chicken stew is just what you want on a cold night. If you don't have fresh shiitake mushrooms on hand, you can replace them with 10 dried shiitakes, soaked in warm water for 30 minutes, drained, stemmed, and sliced, and ¼ pound fresh cremini mushrooms, sliced. Chinese black vinegar, sold in Asian markets, has a flavor not unlike balsamic and, similarly, the quality varies. Look for vinegar with a flavor that is complex and has good depth. The remaining liquid is delicious poured over more rice or noodles for seconds.

SERVES 4

6 skinless chicken thighs, about 2 pounds total

2 teaspoons five-spice powder

1 teaspoon kosher salt

3 tablespoons canola oil

1 tablespoon chopped garlic

1-inch piece fresh ginger, peeled and slivered

3 tablespoons chopped shallot

2 cups chicken broth

2 tablespoons Shaoxing wine

2 tablespoons Chinese black vinegar or balsamic vinegar

1½ teaspoons brown sugar

2 tablespoons soy sauce

½ teaspoon freshly ground pepper

3 whole star anise

½ pound fresh shiitake mushrooms, stemmed and caps sliced (about 3 cups)

1 tablespoon cornstarch dissolved in 2 tablespoons water

½ small head napa cabbage, cored and sliced crosswise into 2-inch-wide pieces

2 green onions, white and green parts, cut into 1-inch matchstick

Rub the chicken thighs with the five-spice powder and salt. In a large, wide pot over medium-high heat, heat 2 tablespoons of the oil. Add the thighs and sear for about 5 minutes on each side, or until lightly brown. Transfer the chicken to a plate, leaving any flavorful browned bits on the bottom of the pot.

In the same pot over medium heat, heat the remaining 1 tablespoon oil. Add the garlic, ginger, and shallot and sauté for 30 seconds until fragrant. Add the broth, wine, vinegar, sugar, soy sauce, and pepper. Bring to a simmer and add the star anise. Return the chicken to the pot, cover, and simmer gently for 30 minutes, or until the chicken is tender. Stir in the mushrooms and cornstarch mixture, re-cover, and continue to cook for another 10 minutes, or until the broth has thickened slightly. Stir in the cabbage and let cook for another 5 minutes, or until wilted.

Remove from the heat and garnish with the green onions just before serving.

thai lemongrass-chili cabbage salad with mixed mushrooms

When I was in college at the University of California at Santa Cruz, my favorite restaurant was India Joze, at the time owned by chef Joseph Schultz. One day I took a class from Schultz on cooking with mushrooms, and this Thai dish is based on one of the recipes out of his little spiral-bound mushroom cookbook. My vegetarian college roommates couldn't get enough of it. If you are a chili lover, turn up the heat and use as many as you can stand.

SERVES 4
as a side dish

½ head green cabbage, cored and slivered
   (about 6 cups)

2 tablespoons kosher salt

2 tablespoons canola oil

½ pound mixed fresh mushrooms such as shiitake,
   oyster, and cremini, stemmed and sliced

5 dried tree ear mushrooms, soaked in hot water
   for 20 minutes, drained, and sliced (optional)

4 teaspoons fish sauce

1 teaspoon sugar

1 teaspoon finely chopped garlic

2 tablespoons finely chopped lemongrass,
   from bottom 4 inches only

1 or 2 Thai or serrano chilies, finely chopped

½ teaspoon freshly ground pepper

2 small red onions, halved and slivered lengthwise

2 tablespoons fresh lime juice, plus 4 lime wedges

2 tablespoons chopped unsalted roasted peanuts

½ cup slivered fresh Thai basil or chopped
   fresh cilantro

In a large bowl, mix together the cabbage and salt. Let stand for 10 minutes, then rinse thoroughly and drain well. Return to the bowl and chill.

In a wok or large, deep skillet over high heat, heat the oil. Add the mushrooms, fish sauce, and sugar and stir-fry for about 2 minutes, or until the mushrooms are tender. Add the garlic, lemongrass, chilies, and pepper and continue stir-frying for 1 minute. Add the onions and stir-fry for 30 seconds more, or until lightly cooked but still crisp.

Remove from the heat and add the lime juice. Toss well and serve over the chilled cabbage. Garnish with the peanuts and cilantro. Serve warm or at room temperature, garnished with the lime wedges.

snow peas and sugar snap peas

Both of these sweet, crunchy peas are edible raw, pod and all. Flat and pale green, snow peas have become so ubiquitous that they're easily found in even the most mainstream markets and appear on the menu of nearly every Chinese restaurant. Snap peas, on the other hand, are not particular to Asian cooking. They are glossier and plumper than snow peas, with thicker skin and tiny developed peas on the inside. I always buy a huge bag of snap peas at the farmers' market and eat half of it on the drive home.

snow peas and sugar snap peas

SELECTING AND STORING: Snow peas are the more delicate of the two, and I often see them in produce sections looking rather tired. Seek out small (and therefore less starchy and more sweet) snow peas that are as crisp as possible, taking into consideration that even at their freshest they might be somewhat flexible. Store snow peas in a loosely closed plastic bag in the refrigerator for no more than 3 days. Firm, crisp snap peas are much more resilient, however, and will last for up to a week.

HOW TO USE: Whether or not snow peas and sugar snap peas need to have the strings removed depends on the batch. If the strings are fibrous just pinch off the stem end and pull the string off with it. Not as sweet and more delicate in texture, snow peas pair particularly well with seafood, but I've also enjoyed them tossed with walnuts. Snap peas are sturdier and can take on beef and pork. Try stir-frying them with an Indian spice trio of cumin, mustard, and fennel seeds.

gado gado

You'll find that even kids love the subtle "peanutty" sweetness of the Indonesian sauce that dresses this traditional salad (it's a good way to get them to eat their vegetables). Although it's not traditional, I prefer to serve the salad as if it were a crudité platter, selecting vegetables that are easy to dip and placing the peanut sauce in a bowl alongside. In addition to, or in place of, the vegetables I've listed here, try cooked red potatoes, blanched long beans, chayote, or lotus root; fresh herbs such as Thai basil and cilantro; or even boiled shrimp. If you can find them, hard-boil tiny quail eggs in place of the chicken eggs for an especially elegant touch.

SERVES 4 TO 6
as an appetizer

VEGETABLES:

½ pound snap peas, trimmed and blanched for 10 seconds

½ pound green beans, trimmed, halved crosswise, and blanched for 1 minute

1 cup bean sprouts, blanched for 10 seconds

2 carrots, peeled and sliced on the diagonal

1 English or Japanese cucumber, sliced

1 bunch watercress, coarse stems removed

3 hard-boiled eggs, peeled and quartered

PEANUT SAUCE:

1 tablespoon peanut or canola oil

1 tablespoon chopped garlic

¼ cup chopped shallot

1 Thai or serrano chili, coarsely chopped

2 teaspoons tamarind concentrate

3 tablespoons fish sauce

1 tablespoon sugar

½ teaspoon ground coriander

¼ teaspoon ground turmeric

¼ cup water

1 cup coconut milk

1 cup unsalted roasted peanuts, finely ground in a food processor

1 tablespoon fresh lemon juice

On a platter, arrange all of the vegetables and hard-boiled eggs decoratively. Cover with plastic wrap and chill.

Meanwhile, make the peanut sauce: In a sauté pan or skillet over medium-low heat, heat the oil. Add the garlic, shallot, and chili and sauté, stirring occasionally, for about 5 minutes, or until the garlic and shallot are browned. Take care not to burn the garlic. Add the tamarind, fish sauce, sugar, coriander, turmeric, and water and sauté for 30 seconds more. Remove from the heat and put the mixture into a food processor or blender. Blend until almost smooth.

Using the same pan over medium heat, bring the coconut milk to a gentle simmer. Add the blended spice mixture and stir to incorporate. Add the ground peanuts and simmer for another 3 to 5 minutes, to marry the flavors. Just before serving, stir in the lemon juice and adjust the consistency of the sauce by adding enough water to make it thick but pourable. Let cool slightly and transfer to a bowl. Serve the sauce warm or at room temperature alongside the vegetables as a dipping sauce.

soybeans

ALSO KNOWN AS: edamame *(Japanese)*

As the Western world gradually embraces dried soybeans in all their forms—miso, tempeh, soy milk, tofu—the young, green fuzzy pods of fresh soybeans are slowly making their way into Western markets, too. Most people are first introduced to fresh soybeans in Japanese restaurants, where they're called *edamame* and are usually boiled, salted, and served in their pods, ready to be popped directly into your mouth. Paired with an icy cold Sapporo, they're the healthiest beer nuts ever. The soybeans you'll find in the market are varieties grown specifically for eating fresh. They're also sold frozen (both in their pods and without) at almost any Asian grocery store and many gourmet markets. My neighbor has found that her kids love them as a snack.

soybeans

SELECTING AND STORING: Soybeans come about three to a pod. I've rarely found them truly fresh. More often, they're sold already parboiled, sometimes labeled "fresh" and sometimes "frozen."

HOW TO USE: The most typical way to enjoy fresh or frozen soybeans is to boil or steam them for about 5 minutes until they just slip right out of their pods, sprinkle them with kosher salt, and eat them then and there. Removed from the pod, I find that their nutty flavor also makes a good substitute for fresh fava beans in most recipes. Try sprinkling them over a salad or tossing them with fried rice.

Richard Wong's tofu with soybeans and mustard greens

SERVES 4
as a side dish

This recipe is typical of Shanghainese cooking, mild and simple, seasoned only with salt, sugar, and sesame oil. Richard buys the preserved mustard greens seasoned with chili paste in a can. They are easily found in a Chinese market.

1 tablespoon kosher salt

¾ pound fresh or frozen soybeans in the pod

¼ pound preserved mustard greens seasoned with chili paste

½ pound Chinese-style firm tofu

1 tablespoon vegetable oil

1 tablespoon sesame oil

1 teaspoon sugar

Bring a large pot filled with water to a boil. Add the salt and soybeans and boil for 5 to 7 minutes, or until the soybeans are cooked through but still a bit crunchy. Drain, and run cold water over them. Shell and set aside.

Cut the mustard greens and tofu into thin, narrow strips about 1 inch long.

In a wok or large, deep skillet over medium heat, heat the vegetable oil. Toss in the greens and tofu and stir-fry gently until warm. Toss in the soybeans and stir-fry until warm. Add the sesame oil and sugar and mix well. Serve at room temperature.

Richard Wong on **soybeans**

Richard Wong was born in Shanghai, but he immigrated to Ohio with his family when he was a child. There, he says, soybeans were mostly used as a throw-away cover crop—certainly not for food. His father, a land developer, cleverly figured out which farmers were planting the beans and would buy them by the bushel directly from the growers. "There weren't many Chinese in Ohio at that time, and the farmers just thought we were crazy," Richard remembers.

Now Richard is the owner of China Blue, a manufacturer of Shanghainese sauces and other food products that are sold at Williams-Sonoma and other upmarket outlets. Fresh soybeans are a large part of Shanghainese cuisine, and Richard uses them like peanuts, sprinkling them on top of dishes at the last minute to add a nutty flavor, texture, and bright chartreuse dots of color. "You barely cook them," Richard says. "Sometimes I'll take pork tenderloin, shred it into very, very thin slivers, season it with red pepper flakes, panfry it until it's crisp and spicy, and throw some soybeans on top. It's beautiful."

edamame with sichuan pepper-salt

Chef Jennifer Cox learned to make Sichuan pepper-salt at San Francisco chef Barbara Tropp's now-closed China Moon Cafe. At her current restaurant, Montage, Jennifer sprinkles it liberally over soybeans—a perfect match. Although many cookbooks call for boiling soybeans, Jennifer prefers to roast them, as she does in this recipe. You will end up with more pepper-salt than you will need, but it's great on everything from stir-fries to roasted meats, and it keeps well in a glass jar for months. If you can't find whole peppercorns, ground Sichuan peppercorns are often sold at Chinese markets. If I don't have the time to make the Sichuan pepper-salt from scratch, I substitute a mix of equal parts of the ground peppercorns and kosher salt.

SERVES 4
as an appetizer

¼ cup Sichuan peppercorns

½ cup kosher salt

1 pound fresh or frozen soybeans in the pod, thawed in the refrigerator if frozen

To make the Sichuan pepper-salt, in a heavy skillet or sauté pan over medium-low heat, toast the peppercorns and salt for about 5 minutes, or until aromatic and the salt turns grayish. The peppercorns may smoke a bit, but that's fine. Remove from the heat and let cool. Process in a food processor until you have a fine powder. Pass through a strainer to remove any unwanted husks.

To prepare the soybeans, preheat the oven to 450°F. Spread them on a baking sheet and sprinkle liberally with the pepper-salt, about 2 tablespoons worth. Roast for 5 to 7 minutes, or until the soybeans are tender but toothsome. Serve warm or at room temperature.

herbs and aromatics

If smell is the most provocative sense, then it's no wonder that herbs and aromatics are among the most characteristic elements of any cuisine. Just as the heady bouquet released by freshly chopped basil and garlic sparks images of Italy, the distinctive fragrance of a handful of lemongrass, chilies, and kaffir lime leaves immediately brings the Thai table to mind. This chapter is an introduction to many of the key seasonings of the Asian pantry. Learn to use them and you're on your way to defining Asian cuisine.

herbs and aromatics

chilies thai, serrano, fresno, jalapeño

It's hard to imagine many Asian cuisines without the heat of chilies. But most sources will tell you that chilies originated in the New World. Countless types exist, but the most common fresh chilies available in Asian markets here are the serrano, fresno, jalapeño, and Thai (the latter also called bird, birdeye, or *prik kee noo*).

Fragrant Thai chilies are one of the true hallmarks of Thai cooking. Following "the smaller the hotter" rule of thumb, they are an inch of pure fire. They range in color from green to orange to red. Look for them in Southeast Asian markets.

The serrano, fresno and jalapeño are also commonly found in Latin and Western markets, and many supermarkets.

chilies, clockwise from top left: jalapeño, fresno, serrano, Thai

SELECTING AND STORING: Chilies should be plump and glossy. Store them in a loosely closed plastic bag in the refrigerator for up to a week. Remember that the color of a chili may tell you its ripeness (green is unripe, red is ripe), but it's not necessarily a good indicator of heat.

HOW TO USE: Although many people will laboriously remove the seeds from chilies before cooking, I chop chilies up, seeds and all, just adding less if necessary. Thai chilies are small enough that you can make a slit lengthwise to release their heat and throw them in whole, cautioning guests to be on the lookout.

When chopping chilies, I slip my hand into a plastic bag, but thin rubber gloves give you more control. As for putting out the flames in your mouth, try a sip of milk, coconut milk, or yogurt, or eat more steamed rice.

pineapple, jicama, and thai chili salsa

MAKES 3 CUPS

Zesty and tropical, this sauce is the perfect addition to a barbecue on a warm summer evening. Try it on top of grilled fish or shrimp. The number of chilies is left up to your mood—or your guests' tolerance. Jicama is a tuber that you'll find in both Latin and Asian markets (where it's sometimes called yam bean). It's mild in taste, somewhat like an apple in texture, and usually peeled and eaten raw. Fresh water chestnuts have similar qualities and would make a good substitute.

1 ½ cups chopped fresh pineapple

1 ½ cups chopped jicama

¼ cup fresh lime juice

½ cup fresh mint leaves, torn into small pieces

4 green onions, white and light green parts, thinly sliced

1 teaspoon sugar

½ teaspoon kosher salt

4 to 10 Thai chilies, finely chopped

In a bowl, combine all the ingredients, cover with plastic wrap, and let stand for at least 1 hour at room temperature or for up to 8 hours refrigerated (the longer the flavors marry, the hotter the salsa will be). Drain and bring to room temperature before serving.

chinese celery

Unlike the brutish stalks Westerners crunch on as a diet snack, Chinese celery is much lankier in appearance and is rarely eaten raw. It varies from light to darker green and looks relatively undeveloped, kind of like a cross between regular celery and Italian parsley. The flavor of Chinese celery is much more concentrated, which makes it more suitable as a flavoring than as a vegetable. You'll rarely find it outside of Asian markets.

chinese celery

SELECTING AND STORING: Look for crisp stems and leaves that aren't yellowing or wilted. Store in a loosely closed plastic bag in the refrigerator for up to 5 days.

HOW TO USE: Once any fibrous strings have been removed, both the stems and leaves can be cooked and eaten. Try stir-frying just the stems with soy sauce, sugar, sesame oil, and cubed tofu. Both the leaves and stems make a good addition to a soup. Bruce Hill, a talented San Francisco chef, takes the classic pairing of fish and celery and cures salmon using Chinese celery as an herb. Cookbook author and chef Ken Hom suggests using it as a swizzle stick for a Bloody Mary.

chinese celery with garlic and lemon zest

MAKES 1 CUP

I like to use Chinese celery like I would Italian parsley. This vibrant green sauce was inspired by the classic northern Italian garnish called gremolada. *It's a two-second pick-me-up for any meat, fish, or even vegetables. Spoon it on pork chops or steamed fish, or toss it with boiled new potatoes.*

½ cup finely chopped Chinese celery leaves
   and stems
1 tablespoon finely chopped lemon zest
2 tablespoons fresh lemon juice
1 tablespoon finely chopped garlic
¼ cup finely chopped shallot
¼ cup canola oil
½ teaspoon kosher salt
Freshly ground pepper to taste

In a bowl, combine all of the ingredients and let sit for 10 minutes before using.

stir-fried catfish with chinese celery and slivered ginger

Southerners consider catfish part of their heritage, but these whiskered fish fill tanks all over Chinatown, too. Almost all store-bought catfish is farm-raised, which eliminates the funky flavors these bottom feeders can have when caught in the wild. Catfish fillets sometimes have a very thin layer of strong-flavored, reddish meat on one side, which is best removed before cooking. Otherwise, the flesh tends to be mild and firm, perfect for stir-frying.

SERVES 4

1¼ pounds catfish fillets

6 tablespoons fresh lime juice

¼ cup oyster sauce

3 tablespoons canola oil

1 to 2 serrano chilies, chopped (optional)

1 teaspoon finely chopped garlic

1 tablespoon peeled slivered ginger

1 cup stemmed and halved cherry tomatoes

1 cup snow peas, trimmed

1 cup sliced fresh shiitake mushrooms

¾ cup chopped Chinese celery leaves and stems

½ teaspoon kosher salt

Cut the catfish into ¼-inch-thick slices and place in a bowl. Combine the lime juice and oyster sauce and mix half of it with the catfish; reserve the remainder for later. Let the catfish marinate for 15 minutes at room temperature.

In a wok or large, deep skillet over high heat, heat 1 tablespoon of the oil. Using a slotted spoon, remove half of the catfish and add it to the pan. Quickly stir-fry for 1 to 2 minutes, or until almost cooked. Transfer the catfish to a bowl, draining off any liquid. Add 1 tablespoon of the oil to the pan and fry the remaining catfish in the same way. Set aside.

Heat the remaining 1 tablespoon oil in the wok over medium-high heat. Add the chili, if using, garlic, and ginger and stir-fry for 10 seconds until fragrant. Add the tomatoes, snow peas, mushrooms, celery leaves and stems, and salt and stir-fry for about 2 minutes, until the mushrooms are tender. Return the catfish slices to the pan and gently toss with the vegetables. Add the reserved lime juice mixture, stir gently, and serve.

chives, garlic green, yellow, flowering

ALSO KNOWN AS: *Chinese chives*

One day while shopping, I was surprised to see an older Eastern European woman at an Asian market buying bunch after bunch of green garlic chives until her arms were full. I asked her what she was going to do with them, and she smiled and said they were destined for a delicious soup. I can imagine it was. Garlic chives at their freshest have a faint, almost sweet, taste of garlic. In the market, you'll find three kinds: green, yellow, and flowering. Yellow chives differ from the green in that they are grown in the dark, have a milder taste, and cost more. Flowering garlic chives have much longer, upright tubular stems with unopened edible buds and are stronger in flavor.

garlic chives, left to right: flowering, green, yellow

SELECTING AND STORING: Green and yellow garlic chives, with their flat leaves, should not be confused with European chives, nor should the latter be substituted for them. Avoid garlic chives that are wilted and have a pungent smell. Flowering chives should be stiff and slightly aromatic. All chives can be stored in a plastic bag in the refrigerator for up to a few days, but don't make the mistake of forgetting you have them, as they can cause quite a stink when they get old!

HOW TO USE: Garlic chives are usually best added to a dish at the last minute. Yellow chives are prized for their color and, in Chinese cooking, are often used in combination with other pale vegetables such as bean sprouts. Try stir-frying chopped yellow and green garlic chives with shrimp and a dash of fish sauce.

curried omelet with ground pork, tomato, and garlic chives

Americans have relegated eggs to breakfast, but they're wonderful any time of the day. This hearty omelet is loosely based on a recipe from Nancie McDermott's Real Thai *cookbook, one of my first introductions to Asian cooking. Served with a green salad, it makes a colorful plate and perfect dinner for popping open a cold, light beer. Makes 2 large omelets.*

SERVES 4

4 eggs

2 tablespoons coconut milk

1 teaspoon curry powder

½ teaspoon kosher salt

¼ teaspoon freshly ground pepper

FILLING:

1 tablespoon canola oil

1 teaspoon finely chopped garlic

¼ cup chopped shallot

½ pound lean ground pork

½ cup chopped tomato

½ cup chopped garlic chives

1 tablespoon fish sauce

½ teaspoon kosher salt

¼ teaspoon sugar

2 teaspoons canola oil

Chili sauce such as *sambal oelek* for dipping (optional)

In a bowl, whisk together the eggs, coconut milk, curry powder, salt, and pepper until blended. Set aside.

To make the filling, in a sauté pan over medium-high heat, heat the oil. Add the garlic and shallot and sauté for 30 seconds until fragrant. Add the ground pork, breaking it up with a spatula as much as possible, and cook, stirring, for another 5 minutes, or until the meat is no longer pink. Drain any fat off and add the tomato, garlic chives, fish sauce, salt, and sugar. Cook, stirring, for another 30 seconds to marry the flavors. Remove from the heat.

In a 10-inch nonstick skillet over medium heat, heat 1 teaspoon of the oil. Pour in half of the egg mixture. Let cook until the edges are beginning to set fully but the center is still slightly runny. Add half of the ground pork mixture to one-half of the omelet and, using a flexible spatula, gently lift up the other half and fold over. Let cook for another 2 minutes.

Tilt the skillet and ease the omelet onto a platter. To make the second omelet, repeat the process with the remaining egg mixture, filling, and oil. Serve immediately with the chili sauce alongside, if desired.

mussels with black beans and flowering garlic chives

Black mussels are readily available in the Bay Area where I live—and cheap at that—but clams also work fine for this dish. It's best to use bivalves the day you purchase them, but if you must store them, keep them refrigerated in a bowl with a damp cloth over them for no longer than a day. Wait to prepare the mussels until you're ready to cook. To clean them, don't submerge them in water. Instead just scrub and rinse each one well to remove any grit. Get rid of any with cracked shells. If you find one gaping open, hold it closed for a second with your fingers. If it won't stay closed, it's likely dead and should be discarded. Some mussels have beards, which look like little "hairs" sticking out the end. To remove them, grip on with your fingers or a dish towel and give a yank. Serve the mussels with crusty bread for sopping up the sauce.

SERVES 4
as a first course

2 tablespoons canola oil

1 teaspoon finely chopped garlic

1 tablespoon peeled and finely chopped
   fresh ginger

2 tablespoons finely chopped shallots

2 tablespoons fermented black beans, chopped

1 cup chicken broth

2 tablespoons Shaoxing wine

1 tablespoon soy sauce

½ teaspoon sugar

2 pounds mussels, cleaned (see recipe introduction)

1 cup chopped flowering garlic chives (1-inch pieces)

4 lemon wedges

In a large wok or pot over medium-high heat, heat the oil. Add the garlic, ginger, shallots, and black beans and cook, stirring, for 1 minute until the shallots are translucent. Add the chicken broth, wine, soy sauce, and sugar and bring to a boil. Add the mussels, reduce the heat to a simmer, cover, and cook for 3 to 4 minutes, or until the mussels have opened. Add the chives, toss to incorporate, cover, and cook for 30 seconds more to cook the chives.

Using tongs, transfer the mussels to bowls, discarding any that failed to open. Ladle a bit of the broth into each bowl. Accompany each serving with a wedge of lemon.

curry leaves

ALSO KNOWN AS: *kari leaves*

Although these aromatic leaves are sometimes used in Sri Lankan and Malaysian cooking, they're an integral part of south Indian cuisine and are often sold prepackaged in plastic bags at Indian markets. They're not always available, however, so when you find them, you should snap them up. Typically, ten or more fragile, pointy leaves, approximately the size of a small bay leaf, grow from a central stem. Dried leaves are available, but, not surprisingly, they can't measure up to the fresh. Don't be tempted by the curry plants you'll find in Western nurseries. They are not the same thing.

curry leaves

SELECTING AND STORING: Fresh curry leaves are generally kept in plastic bags in the refrigerated section of an Indian market, although I've also seen them sitting out at room temperature. They should be shiny, dark green, and fragrant when crushed. Slipped into a plastic bag, they will keep for at least a week. I always buy more than I plan to use, and freeze the others in a lock-top bag. They will last nicely for at least a couple months.

HOW TO USE: Whole sprigs of fresh curry leaves are often quickly fried (because they can burn in seconds) in ghee or oil with other Indian spices such as mustard seeds and cumin and then stirred into a dal. They're delicious with chopped tomatoes or fresh corn kernels. Try chopping the leaves and adding them to scrambled eggs, or grinding them with coconut, chilies, and tamarind to make a chutney.

soupy dal with curry leaves and lemon

In India, dal refers to a wide variety of dried legumes (often called pulses) such as lentils, peas, and mung beans, but it also is used for the prepared dish. Typically, the legumes are first simmered without any spices. Only after they're cooked does the magic come in: salt is added, and spices— from cumin seeds to mustard seeds—are fried up in a generous amount of ghee or oil and poured over the legumes. I favor chana dal, *the deep yellow, meaty, split chickpeas (garbanzo beans), for this recipe, but yellow split peas can replace them as long as you shorten the cooking time. Rather than remove the curry leaves from their sprigs (if they're still attached), leave them intact, so that they're more easily removed when you're ready to eat. Make a pot of basmati rice or a stack of chapatis to serve along with the dal.*

SERVES 4 TO 6
as a side dish

½ pound *chana dal* (about 1¼ cups)

4 cups water

½ teaspoon ground turmeric

2 thin slices fresh ginger

1 teaspoon kosher salt

2 teaspoons garam masala

2 tablespoons fresh lemon juice

3 tablespoons canola oil

1 teaspoon cumin seeds

2 sprigs fresh curry leaves (about 20 leaves total)

In a pot over high heat, bring the *chana dal* and water to a boil. Reduce the heat to low and simmer, skimming the white foam off the top with a spoon. When the majority of the foam is removed, stir in the turmeric and ginger and cover the pot. Cook for 45 to 60 minutes, or until the legumes are tender and the dal is still soupy and rather thin. Remove from the heat and stir in the salt, garam masala, and lemon juice.

In a small sauté pan over medium-high heat, heat the oil. Add the cumin seeds, and when they start to sizzle and pop, after about 30 seconds, add the curry leaves. Fry for a few more seconds, taking care not to allow the leaves to burn, then pour the contents of the pan over the dal. Stir to incorporate and serve at once.

galangal and turmeric

GALANGAL ALSO KNOWN AS: laos *(Indonesian), Siamese ginger, Thai ginger*

Although these rhizomes are used in very different ways, both galangal and turmeric deserve more attention. Stockier in size, galangal is fiery—almost bitter—in taste compared to ginger. It has telltale rings wrapping around muscular knobs to the point of looking almost woody. Turmeric, on the other hand, is usually about as thick as your first finger, with a comparatively mild flavor. It may look drab and brown on the outside, but on the inside it's vibrant orange (the same color as its dried and ground form). Look for both rhizomes in Southeast Asian markets and turmeric in Indian stores.

galangal (top) and turmeric (on plate)

SELECTING AND STORING: There is no need to peel galangal, but do look for smaller specimens that are easier to slice, with no signs of mold. Store it in a paper bag in the refrigerator. Turmeric is often sold in little bags with air holes. Kept in this bag in the refrigerator, it will store well for 2 weeks.

HOW TO USE: Galangal should be used in small doses. It is crucial to much of Thai cooking, where it is eaten slivered raw in squid salad, thinly sliced and tossed in hot-and-sour soup, and added to green curry paste. Turmeric gives yellow curry its sunshine color (as well as most anything it touches). In Southern Thai cooking it's pounded with garlic to make a paste for fried catfish. To make Indonesian yellow coconut rice, infuse chopped fresh turmeric in simmering water for 5 minutes. Strain and add the turmeric water and coconut milk to rice that has been sauteed with cloves, cardamom, and pieces of lemongrass. Season, cover, and steam until done.

thai coconut chicken soup with galangal and lime leaves

When you make this classic chicken soup, the kaffir lime leaves, lemongrass, and lime infuse your house with a heavenly smell of citrus that lures everyone into the kitchen. It's a quick soup to make because very little chopping is involved. Many things need to be "bruised," however, which just means giving them a whack with the blunt side of your knife to release the flavor. Remind your guests to eat around the galangal, lemongrass, lime leaves, and chili to avoid rude surprises. Serve small portions as a beginning to a meal or make it the main course.

SERVES 4 TO 6
as a first course

3 cups coconut milk

2 ½ cups chicken broth

1 ½-inch piece galangal, cut into about 15 thin slices and bruised

3 lemongrass stalks, bottom 4 inches only, tough outer leaves removed, halved crosswise, and bruised

3 kaffir lime leaves, lightly crushed

½ teaspoon freshly ground pepper

1 Thai chili, slit lengthwise halfway to expose the flesh

2 tablespoons plus 2 teaspoons fish sauce

1 teaspoon sugar

¾ pound boneless, skinless chicken thigh meat (about 4 thighs), cut into 1-inch pieces

6 fresh shiitake mushrooms, stemmed and sliced

½ red onion, thinly sliced crosswise (about 1 cup)

Fresh lime juice to taste

Chopped fresh cilantro for garnish

In a pot over medium heat, heat together the coconut milk and broth. Add the galangal, lemongrass, lime leaves, pepper, and chili and bring to a simmer. Reduce the heat to as low as possible and cook for 10 minutes to infuse the flavors.

Add the fish sauce and sugar and stir well. Add the chicken and simmer for 5 minutes, or until the chicken is opaque. Add the mushrooms and onion and cook for 5 minutes more, making sure the chicken is cooked through. Add the lime juice to taste. The soup should have a lively balance of sweet, sour, and salty. Adjust, adding more sugar, lime juice, or fish sauce as necessary. Ladle into bowls, garnish with the cilantro, and serve immediately.

ginger

It's not until you go to a Chinatown market that you realize the extent to which ginger is used in Asian cooking. No one is breaking off little one-inch pieces to bring home for the week. People buy huge "hands" of it. The recipes in this book call for common mature ginger, but you'll also run across young ginger (sometimes called stem ginger) in Asian markets. Young ginger is just that—harvested before the papery, light brown skin has formed. It is similar in size, is a lovely ivory with a tinge of pink, and has more tender flesh. Oddly, instead of being milder, I find young ginger can have more of a kick.

new ginger (bottom), mature ginger (top)

SELECTING AND STORING: Look for ginger with smooth, unwrinkled skin. When cut into, it should have creamy-colored, relatively unfibrous flesh with no sign of browning. Mature ginger can be stored in a paper bag in the refrigerator for up to 3 weeks, while young ginger should be used within the week.

HOW TO USE: If you are making a refined dish, I recommend peeling ginger. Otherwise, if it's sliced or chopped very finely, the skin can be left on. It's impossible even to begin to count the ways ginger is used all over Asia: slivered along with green onions and steamed on top of fish, used in curries, pickled. A tea made with fresh ginger, honey, cayenne, and lemon is what my mother prescribes when I'm sick, and an Indian friend purees ginger with garlic and a little water to have on hand when there's last-minute cooking to be done.

carrot-ginger soup

SERVES 4

This pureed vegetarian soup shows off two old friends: carrots and ginger. Don't even consider using those tired, bitter carrots that have been in the bottom of the refrigerator for two weeks. Prepare it in the summer when carrots are being plucked right from the ground and are crunchy and sweet. If you don't care whether or not it's vegetarian, you can replace the vegetable broth with chicken broth. Try garnishing the soup with a sprinkle of chopped cilantro and grated carrot.

¼ cup unsalted butter

2 tablespoons minced fresh ginger

4 teaspoons finely chopped garlic

1 to 2 serrano chilies, coarsely chopped

3 cups vegetable broth

2 pounds carrots, peeled and cut into chunks

¼ teaspoon ground coriander

1 teaspoon kosher salt

¾ cup half-and-half

In a pot over medium heat, melt the butter. Add the ginger, garlic, and chili and cook for about 30 seconds until fragrant. Add the vegetable broth, bring to a simmer, and add the carrots, coriander, and salt. Cover and cook for 20 to 25 minutes, or until the carrots are very soft.

Working in batches, if necessary, pour the soup into a blender and puree until perfectly smooth. Return the mixture to the pot and add the half-and-half. Return the soup to a simmer over low heat. Adjust the consistency by adding a little water, if necessary. Ladle into bowls and serve hot.

herbs

A whole array of everyday and esoteric herbs crucial to Asian cooking exists and the following are the most common ones.

BASIL, THAI

Two different kinds of basil play a large part in Southeast Asian cooking: Thai basil and holy basil. The first one is a signature Thai herb used in Vietnamese and Laotian cooking, too. The leaves are tinged purple, as are its stems. The aroma is unforgettable, a combination of basil, licorice, and mint. The Thais add big handfuls of whole leaves to stir-fries. The latter, holy basil (not pictured), is less common. Beloved by Thais, its slightly hairy green leaves have a matte finish and are more jagged, and it has a more spicy flavor with a minty scent. As opposed to sweet basil, which is often eaten raw in salads, holy basil tastes best cooked.

CILANTRO *Chinese parsley, coriander*

Cilantro needs little introduction, as it's one of the most popular herbs East to West. I've seen people confuse it with Italian parsley because of its similarly shaped leaves, but just give it a sniff and you'll know what's in your hands. Cilantro has a slightly earthy, herbaceous scent, and in Asian cooking, every part of it is used, from the whole seeds (coriander) to the roots, which are pounded and added to curry pastes.

MINT

The same variety of spearmint that Westerners use to garnish desserts adds a refreshing sparkle to a variety of savory Asian dishes. Thais use mint in salads, Indians make a delicious chutney with it, and it's a standard ingredient in fresh Vietnamese spring rolls. Look for the smallest, most tender leaves and don't overdo it—a little goes a long way.

RAU RAM *Cambodian mint, hot mint,* laksa *leaf (Malay), Vietnamese mint*

This popular Southeast Asian herb has small, slender green leaves imprinted with a faint black mark. *Rau ram* has a grassy scent with a vaguely soapy flavor that is something of an acquired taste. The Vietnamese love it in salads and fresh spring rolls, and it plays an essential role in *laksa,* the seafood-noodle soup of Malaysia and Singapore. *Rau Ram* is never cooked, but rather eaten raw or tossed into a soup at the very last minute.

SHISO *Perilla, beefsteak plant*

This pretty herb has relatively large leaves with distinctive jagged edges and an anise-like flavor. Two kinds are available, red and green (with some in between). Both are used in Japanese cooking: rolled up in sushi, used as a wrap for pieces of cooked meat and seafood, coated and fried for tempura. The Vietnamese use *shiso* in similar ways, often adding it raw to a salad.

herbs, clockwise from top left: mint, shiso, cilantro, Thai basil, rau ram

SELECTING AND STORING: With all herbs, look for fresh leaves that aren't crushed or slimy. Although some people store herbs stems down in water in the refrigerator, I find that this can make their leaves turn black from getting too cold. I prefer to store them, unwashed and dry, in a loosely closed plastic bag in the refrigerator.

HOW TO USE: Most herbs are best when lightly chopped and are usually best when added to a dish at the very end of cooking, so that they maintain their vibrant flavor.

thai spicy basil chicken

I find I can't get enough of the heavenly bouquet of Thai basil, and I often end up adding twice the amount called for in this recipe. Although I always prefer dark meat for its richer flavor and moistness, you can use boneless, skinless breasts or chicken tenders in its place. Try to chop the chicken as finely as possible. Ground chicken or turkey is an easy alternative. Proceed with caution if you choose to add the Thai chilies at the end. Use a mix of red and green for a boost of color.

SERVES 4

3 tablespoons canola oil

2 tablespoons finely chopped garlic

1½ teaspoons finely chopped Thai or serrano chili

1 pound boneless, skinless chicken thighs, chopped into small pieces

3 tablespoons fish sauce

1 teaspoon soy sauce

½ teaspoon sugar

2 red Thai chilies, thinly sliced on the diagonal into ovals (optional)

1 firmly packed cup Thai sweet basil leaves

In a wok or large, deep skillet over high heat, heat the oil. Add the garlic and stir-fry for 15 seconds until fragrant. Add the Thai or serrano chili and stir-fry for 15 seconds more. Add the chicken and stir-fry for about 1 minute, or until it becomes opaque. Add the fish sauce, soy sauce, and sugar and continue to stir-fry for about 2 minutes, or until the chicken is cooked through.

Remove from the heat and toss with the sliced chilies, if using, and the basil until the basil leaves wilt. Turn out onto a platter immediately and serve to keep the basil leaves from losing their bright green color.

Charles Phan's fresh spring rolls with turmeric fish and rau ram

Although fresh spring rolls are sold at many Vietnamese restaurants, they're often tough and tasteless. Making them at home is a lot of work, but well worth the effort. Charles fondly remembers eating at a small spot in Hanoi where they offered only two things: water snails stewed with herbs and fish-filled spring rolls. At his restaurant, he makes his own version of the rolls, using Mekong Basa, a Vietnamese catfish that is hard to find in retail fish markets. Any firm white fish, such as snapper, domestic catfish, or even halibut, will work as a substitute. The recipe makes more dipping sauce than you'll need. Transfer any extra to a jar with a lid and refrigerate for up to a week or more. Makes about 20 rolls.

SERVES 10
as an appetizer

MARINADE:

1 tablespoon fish sauce

2 teaspoons ground turmeric

1 teaspoon minced garlic

1 teaspoon minced fresh ginger

¼ cup canola oil

1¾ pounds fish fillets such as Mekong Basa or
   other firm white fish (see recipe introduction)

3 ounces rice vermicelli (about ¼ package)

DIPPING SAUCE:

¼ cup fish sauce

¼ cup rice vinegar

¼ cup sugar

¼ cup water

2 tablespoons fresh lime juice

2 teaspoons finely chopped garlic

3 to 6 Thai chilies, minced

2 tablespoons canola oil

20 rice paper rounds, 6 inches in diameter

1 head red leaf lettuce, leaves deribbed and torn
   into 20 small pieces each about 2 by 4 inches

1 bunch *rau ram*, about 20 sprigs, leaves detached

To make the marinade, in a bowl, combine all the ingredients, mixing well. Add the fish, turn to coat evenly, and allow to marinate at room temperature for 20 minutes.

Meanwhile, soak the rice noodles in a bowl of warm water for 20 minutes, or until soft. Bring a pot filled with water to a boil. Drain the noodles, add to the boiling water, and cook for 30 to 60 seconds, or until just tender. Drain and rinse under cold running water to cool. Use kitchen scissors to cut the noodles roughly into manageable pieces. Set aside.

To make the dipping sauce, in a bowl, combine all of the ingredients for the dipping sauce, mixing well. Set aside.

In a nonstick skillet over medium-high heat, heat the oil. Add the fish to the skillet and sear for about 3 minutes on the first side. Turn and cook for about 3 minutes longer, or until opaque in the center. Transfer to a plate lined with doubled paper towels. Cut the fish into thin strips (don't worry if it breaks up a bit).

Fill a pie tin or other shallow container with warm water. Spread out a clean dish towel on the table. Dip a sheet of rice paper into the warm water for about 3 seconds, until it is just beginning to become pliable. Place the sheet flat on the towel and allow to sit for another few seconds until it is completely soft. If it does not soften, rub your wet fingers along any parts that are still hard.

Lay 1 piece of lettuce over the bottom third of the rice paper. Lay a small amount of rice noodle on top of the lettuce, then a few *rau ram* leaves, and then finally a strip of fish. Fold the left and then the right side over the filling. Starting from the edge near you, fold the rice paper halfway over the filling, and then roll up into a tight cylinder. It will seal naturally. Repeat until all the rolls are made, placing them on a platter and covering them with a damp towel so they will stay moist.

Arrange the rolls on a platter and serve with the dipping sauce alongside.

Charles Phan on **rau ram**

A sleek interior, smart wine list, and, most of all, wonderful Vietnamese country cooking continues to make Charles Phan's restaurant, The Slanted Door, one of the hottest reservations in San Francisco. Although the Vietnamese use quite an assortment of herbs, *rau ram* is the herb Charles uses most. "It's used in Vietnam as much as basil is here," says Charles. "But ten years ago, it was impossible to find it in the United States. Someone gave my mother a stem to grow and that was our only source." Far easier to come by now, little bundles of it are sold in many Asian markets. Charles uses *rau ram* in his signature grapefruit salad, and you'll see flecks of it in his beef carpaccio drizzled with green onion oil and lime juice and scattered with chopped peanuts. *Rau ram* is never cooked, Charles warns. "The Vietnamese use herbs very delicately." In soup, the leaves are eaten whole and just the heat of the soup wilts them. If you are chopping *rau ram*, he advises a light hand.

kaffir lime leaves

Anyone who has eaten Thai food will have seen these little citrus leaves floating in a bowl of curry. Like lemongrass, they are the essence of Thai cooking and are irreplaceable. A whole kaffir lime leaf is glossy and dark green and looks a bit like botanical Siamese twins: two leaves attached at their tips. By the time it reaches a market, though, the leaves have often been separated. The tree itself is short and the thick and bumpy kaffir fruits that grow from it are used mostly for their peel. Although the fresh limes are sometimes available too, the leaves are more commonly found (often imported from Hawaii) at a market that caters to a Southeast Asian clientele. Some folks have luck growing the tree, which can be obtained through upscale catalogs like Shepherd's Garden Seeds. But in foggy San Francisco, my poor sprig never grew me enough leaves for one bowl of soup!

kaffir lime leaves

SELECTING AND STORING: Kaffir lime leaves are usually sold in small bags holding only a single ounce. I recommend buying more than you immediately need and freezing the rest in a lock-top bag. They will last this way for a few months.

HOW TO USE: Just scratch a kaffir lime leaf and its enticing citrusy fragrance will go straight to your head. You don't need to add too many leaves to a dish to get its effect. Crush them in your hand to release their oils and throw them into a soup (see page 129 for recipe) or curry, or remove the center rib, sliver the leaves, and stir-fry them with rice or toss them into a salad.

lemongrass

When chefs started infusing lemongrass into crème brûlée, I knew lemongrass had crossed the border for good. How could someone not love its bright, citrusy flavors, especially since it has none of the sourness of lemon? When it's growing, lemongrass is tall and has long grassy leaves, but it's usually sold trimmed to its fibrous, most flavorful stalk. In many mainstream markets, you'll find it in the "exotics" section, but unfortunately it's often emaciated and dry. In Asian markets, where there's a good turnover, you'll choose from a bounty of fat, fresh stalks. You can even try rooting a stalk in water and planting it in full sun and sandy soil: in subtropical Louisiana, where my parents live, lemongrass grows effortlessly in their backyard.

lemongrass

SELECTING AND STORING: Look for lemongrass stalks that are plump at the base and not too dry. Store in a loosely closed plastic bag in the refrigerator for up to 2 weeks.

HOW TO USE: Lemongrass can be used all the way up to where the leaves begin to grow, but I usually use only the last 4 inches or so of the stalk (measuring from the root end). Trim off the bottom, and you'll see some beautiful concentric circles of purple inside. Keep removing the outer layers of stalk until you get down to the least fibrous part (this may be a few layers) and you're ready to go. Slice lemongrass as thinly as possible before mincing it, then add to a salad, or cut into 2-inch pieces on the diagonal and bruise it with the back of a knife to release the oils, then add it to a soup or curry. For the ultimate fresh lemonade, try infusing pieces of lemongrass with lemon juice, sweeten with sugar syrup, and top off with sparkling water.

grilled lemongrass-tamarind pork chops with chayote slaw

My parents have grilled every Sunday since I can remember, and they came up with this recipe. The blended paste imparts a citrusy fragrance to the smoky pork chops, and it's so simple that it makes a great work-night dinner, especially if you've made the paste ahead of time. If you have leftovers, the pork and slaw make a great sandwich. If you don't have time to start the grill, you can also sear the chops in a skillet and finish them in a 400°F oven.

SERVES 4

MARINADE:

8 lemongrass stalks, bottom 4 inches only, tough
  outer leaves removed and minced

1 tablespoon finely chopped garlic

1 small yellow onion, quartered

2 tablespoons tamarind concentrate

1 teaspoon kosher salt

4 pork chops, about 1 1/2 inches thick

CHAYOTE SLAW

1 chayote, peeled, seeded, and cut into 1/2-inch cubes

1/2 pound napa cabbage (about 1/4 head), cored and
  chopped into 1/2-inch pieces

1 cup sugar snap peas, trimmed and cut on the
  diagonal into 1-inch pieces

2 carrots, peeled and cut on the diagonal into
  1/4-inch-thick slices

1/2 red onion, thinly sliced

1/4 cup mayonnaise

3 tablespoons rice vinegar

1 teaspoon sugar

1/2 teaspoon kosher salt

1/4 cup slivered fresh Thai basil

To make the marinade, in a food processor or blender, combine all of the ingredients and puree to form a fairly smooth paste. Slather the paste on both sides of each pork chop. Cover and refrigerate for at least 30 minutes or for up to 1 hour. Bring to room temperature before grilling.

To make the chayote slaw, in a large bowl, combine the chayote, cabbage, snap peas, carrots, and onion. In a small bowl, whisk together the mayonnaise, vinegar, sugar, and salt. Pour the mayonnaise mixture over the vegetables and toss to mix. (The salad can now sit for up to an hour or so before serving.) Toss with the Thai basil and set aside.

Meanwhile, prepare a fire in a charcoal grill. When the coals are hot, place the pork chops on the grill rack and sear on each side for 2 minutes, or until they are nice and brown. Move the chops away from directly over the coals and continue to grill for about 15 minutes, or until cooked through (a blush of pink in the center is desirable). Serve immediately with the chayote slaw.

pantry glossary

BEAN SAUCE One whole aisle of a large Asian market could easily be dedicated to the multitude of soybean products, and bean sauces are among the most common. Even the most experienced cook can be intimidated by the numerous variations on this salty condiment. You'll see jars labeled as everything from yellow bean paste and brown bean sauce to black bean–garlic sauce. If you look closely, you'll see that some are made with mashed whole beans and some are pureed. For something all-purpose, look for plain "bean sauce," which should have whole beans (you can actually see them through the glass jar sometimes), and therefore more texture. Koon Chun and Lee Kum Kee are reliable brands.

BLACK BEANS, FERMENTED See Fermented black beans.

CHICKEN BROTH I'd like to think that everyone stays home on weekends to labor lovingly over a pot of simmering chicken broth, but few people—including me—have the time. I use Pacific brand organic chicken broth for its mild flavor and its carton, rather than can, infusing it as necessary when I'm making soups. You may, of course, use a canned broth as well, preferably a low-sodium one. But if you do have an afternoon free, it's satisfying to make your own unsalted broth and freeze it in practical-sized portions. This simple unsalted broth makes a good base for most Asian recipes. You can add salt, soy sauce, or fish sauce, or infuse it with more aromatics such as lemongrass and ginger as necessary.

CHILI SAUCE Numerous Asian chili sauces are on the market, but my favorite is *sambal oelek* (actually labeled chili paste), an Indonesian type made from chilies, salt, and vinegar. (Some manufacturers use the more contemporary spelling *sambal ulek*.) Although it's fiery, it's tolerable enough to serve on the side for dipping, and it enlivens any stir-fry or soup. For an excellent version, look for a plastic container with a rooster on it and a green lid. Made by Huy Fong Foods, it's readily available in Asian and many Western markets. If it doesn't suit you or you can't find it, experiment with other chili sauces to see what you like best.

CHINESE SAUSAGE Made from either pork, beef, or duck, these mild, slightly sweet sausages are flecked with fat and resemble a candlestick-thin salami. You can find them vacuum packed or hanging by strings above the meat counter in many Asian markets or in stores specializing in dried goods. Chinese sausage is typically steamed before using, or sliced and added to a dish while it cooks. It is never eaten cold.

COCONUT MILK There's no need to start hammering at a fresh coconut in order to capture the watery liquid inside. That's not coconut milk in any case, but rather a clear liquid that is drunk as a refreshing beverage and is sometimes used in cooking. Coconut milk is made by soaking the grated flesh of a coconut in hot water and then straining the combination. Canned unsweetened coconut milk is perfectly acceptable and much easier. If the recipe calls for coconut cream, simply skim the layer of cream off the top of an unshaken can. Otherwise, shake the can thoroughly before opening it, in order to mix the milk and cream together. Once opened, refrigerate coconut milk in glass or plastic and use within 2 to 3 days. Chaokoh from Thailand is a reliable brand.

CORIANDER   One of the predominant spices in Indian, Thai, and Indonesian cooking, lemony-tasting coriander is the seed of the coriander—or the cilantro—plant. For optimal aroma and flavor, store the seeds whole and grind as necessary in a spice grinder or clean coffee grinder.

CORNSTARCH   Cornstarch is used as a thickener in Asian cooking, especially Chinese. When used correctly, it adds a suppleness and an attractive sheen to sauces. When used improperly, it makes a goopy mess. It is never added directly to dishes, however. Instead, dissolve it in water or other cold liquid such as chicken broth in the ratio of 1 part cornstarch to 2 parts liquid, and incorporate it toward the end of cooking, allowing anywhere from 15 seconds to a minute or so for the sauce to thicken. If your cornstarch mixture has sat for a bit and settled, give it a quick stir before adding it to a dish.

CUMIN   Cumin—both whole seeds and ground—is one of the most popular spices in Indian cooking. The cumin that you buy in Western markets is usually a Latin variety and perfectly acceptable, while the cumin seeds sold in Indian markets tend to be shorter and fatter and some cooks think more flavorful. You'll also find black cumin seeds in Indian markets, but these shouldn't be substituted for regular brown seeds. For optimal aroma and flavor, store the seeds whole and grind as necessary in a spice grinder or clean coffee grinder.

CURRY PASTE, THAI   Thai curry pastes are made from an assortment of fresh aromatics such as lemongrass, galangal, and chilies that are pounded or ground together. They should not be confused with the makings of an Indian curry, which is typically dried spices slow-cooked with onions, ginger, garlic, and sometimes tomato. Homemade Thai curry pastes yield the best flavor, but they are a lot of effort and store-bought pastes are completely acceptable—even very good. Having them on hand means that you can whip up a Thai curry with a moment's notice. Look for Mae Ploy, a popular brand sold in small tubs. Your choices are usually yellow, red, or green curry paste.

CURRY POWDER   The mix of ground spices we know as curry powder is typically a blend of turmeric (which gives it its yellow color), cinnamon, cumin, coriander, cardamom, cloves, ginger, and red pepper. But a proper curry is always made with a blend of spices (called a *masala*) that is determined by the dish being cooked. If you're just looking for a quick fix, however, it's always better to buy premade curry powder from an Indian market than off the spice shelf of your local supermarket.

DRIED MUSHROOMS   The most common dried mushrooms in the Asian market are shiitakes, also known as Chinese black mushrooms. In Western markets they are available in tiny—and pricey— 2- to 8-ounce bags, but in Asian markets and apothecaries they are packaged in large cellophane sacks or boxes and are sold at varying prices, depending on the quality of the mushrooms. Shiitakes also vary in appearance and size: some caps are smooth and some have white cracks (and are considered to be superior). Dried tree ear mushrooms are also sold in Asian markets. To use, soak dried mushrooms in warm water to cover for about 30 minutes, or until softened; remove any hard stems. The water used to soak dried mushrooms makes a flavorful addition to a soup or sauce. Stored in a sealed plastic bag, dried mushrooms will keep in the cupboard for at least 6 months.

DRIED SHRIMP   These nibble-sized, salty dried shrimp are used in varying sizes as flavoring agents. The smaller ones can be fried and used as a seasoning, but the larger ones need to be soaked in hot water for 15 minutes before using. Dried shrimp are sold in plastic bags and may be kept in a cool place or refrigerated. Look for ones that are bright pinkish orange. Pass up those with a gray cast.

FERMENTED BLACK BEANS   These soft but dry, fermented black soybeans (also known as salted black beans and preserved black beans) are used sparingly for their salty, slightly yeasty flavor. They can enhance everything from steamed fish to stir-fried greens to steamed spareribs. Some cooks rinse the beans before using them, but there seems to be little point to this, as it diminishes their flavor. Pearl River Bridge brand, easily identifiable by its yellow cardboard canister and the brand I use, puts ginger in its black beans. You'll also find fermented black beans sold in plastic bags. Transfer to a clean airtight jar and store indefinitely.

FISH SAUCE   Whether it's called *nuoc mam* in Vietnam or *nam pla* in Thailand, fish sauce is the soy sauce of Southeast Asia. Salty and savory, this amber liquid, made from fermented anchovies or other small fish, is sold in both glass and plastic bottles. Soy sauce can be used in its place, but it's saltier and sharper in taste and will give your dish a very different flavor. More expensive fish sauces (although rarely over five dollars) are usually from the first press, and, like a good olive oil, are used for dipping sauces rather than cooking. Look for Viet Huong's Three Crabs brand. Fish sauce will keep indefinitely in a cool, dry place.

FIVE-SPICE POWDER Five-spice powder is a Chinese spice blend which typically includes star anise, fennel, Sichuan peppercorns, cloves, and cinnamon, although licorice root and ginger sometimes turn up as well. As with any ground spice, it should be kept in a cool, dark place and used within a year.

GARAM MASALA Garam masala is a blend of Indian spices. While many cooks prefer to make their own, it is possible to buy perfectly good prepared mixtures at Indian markets. But if you wish to grind your own for the freshest flavor, try this combination:

2 tablespoons cumin seeds

2 tablespoons coriander seeds

1 tablespoon peppercorns

2 teaspoons cardamom seeds (not the whole pods)

$^3/_4$ teaspoon whole cloves

1 cinnamon stick, about 3 inches long, broken into smaller pieces

Finely grind all the ingredients in a spice grinder or clean coffee grinder. The mixture will keep for about a month or two in an airtight container on a dark shelf.

HOISIN SAUCE This mahogany-colored sauce varies from scoop-it-out-thick to pourable. It owes its big flavor—sweet, salty, tangy—to a varying mixture of soybeans, sugar, garlic, sesame seeds, vinegar, and chilies. In addition to being used as a cooking ingredient, it's served alongside Peking duck and mu shu pork. Once opened, it should be stored in the refrigerator, where it will keep for several months. Koon Chun is a recommended brand.

HOT-PEPPER PASTE, KOREAN See Korean hot-pepper powder, red pepper flakes, and hot-pepper paste.

KOREAN HOT-PEPPER POWDER, RED PEPPER FLAKES, AND HOT-PEPPER PASTE You know Koreans like it hot when you see finely ground red pepper powder and roughly ground red pepper flakes sold by the pound! Hot, but not outrageously so, and slightly sweet, these Korean staples can be interchanged if necessary, but have no real substitute. Both should be kept in tightly sealed containers in a dark, cool spot. Hot-pepper paste, made from sweet rice, hot-pepper powder, and soybeans, is usually sold in glass jars and is brick-red, smooth, and thick. It makes a great addition to any grilling marinade. All of these ingredients are readily found at Korean markets.

KOSHER SALT See Salt, kosher.

MIRIN Used in Japanese cooking, mirin is sweetened sake (rice wine). It is never drunk as a beverage, nor should it be substituted for drinking sake when called for in a recipe. It's used to add a mildly sweet flavor to broths, marinades, and noodles and is an essential flavoring in teriyaki sauces. Kikkoman is a common brand. Refrigerate once opened.

MISO Full of protein and a staple of Japanese and Korean pantries, miso paste is made by salting soybeans and fermenting them with a grain such as rice or barley. A variety of misos are available, identified by their colors, such as white (*shiro-miso*) and red (*aka-miso*). Misos also vary depending on the amount of salt used. They are often stocked in the refrigerated section of Japanese markets, health food stores, and gourmet grocers, in 1-pound plastic bags or tubs. Once opened, store miso in a tightly sealed plastic bag in the refrigerator and it will keep indefinitely. Miso is made into soups, but it's also used to flavor marinades and salad dressings.

MUSHROOMS, DRIED See Dried mushrooms.

MUSTARD SEEDS Frequently used in Indian cooking, mustard seeds come in a few colors: yellow (most often found in Western markets, but not preferred for Indian cooking), brown (the best all-purpose choice), and black (often used for pickling). To make matters confusing, brown mustard seeds are often labeled as black mustard seeds in Indian markets. It's best to identify them by their color, which ranges from purplish black to dark brown. When cooking with mustard seeds, first fry them in hot oil until they pop; this keeps them from being bitter. If you are using a shallow pan, take care to cover it, or you'll have tiny mustard seeds all over your floor.

NOODLES

CELLOPHANE NOODLES Also called mung bean, bean thread, glass, or silver noodles, these dried noodles are made from mung bean starch. They are usually as skinny as angel hair (although I have seen thicker versions) and are often sold in small bundles bound with string. Unless you are deep-frying cellophane noodles, they need to be soaked in hot water for 20 minutes, or until softened, before using. When cooked, they become slithery and clear.

NOODLES, FRESH Golden yellow fresh Chinese egg noodles come in many sizes, from thick (usually called chow mein or lo mein) to thin (usually called wonton). They are found in the refrigerated section of Asian and some Western markets and are ideal for soups and stir-fries. Made without eggs, thick and chewy Shanghai-style noodles are paler in color and are generally used in stir-fries and less often in soups. To cook fresh noodles, loosen them, drop into a generous pot of boiling water, stir, and cook for about 3 minutes, depending on their size. Drain, rinse with water, and toss with oil if necessary to keep from sticking. A 1-pound package should serve 4 to 6 people. Fresh noodles will keep in the refrigerator for 3 to 5 days, but I always buy more than I need at the time and freeze the rest. The frozen noodles do not need to be defrosted before cooking. Just start counting the minutes once the water returns to a boil.

RICE NOODLES, DRIED These slightly translucent white noodles are made with rice flour. Two basic kinds are sold: rice vermicelli (skinny like *spaghettini*) and rice sticks (flat and ranging from the size of linguine to about twice that). Unless you are deep-frying them, dried rice noodles should be soaked in hot water for 20 minutes, or until softened, before using. They will turn opaque when cooked.

SWEET POTATO NOODLES, DRIED I'd trade the most supple linguine in the world for a bowl of the pleasingly chewy, magically translucent sweet potato noodles, also known as Korean vermicelli. Look for them in Korean markets or mail order them (see Sources). Soak them in hot water for 20 minutes, or until softened, before using. The more common cellophane noodles can be substituted, but seek out those that are thicker than angel hair.

OYSTER SAUCE Oyster sauce is made with oyster extract, sugar, salt, and sometimes MSG. It's dark brown, very salty, and somewhat sweet. Quality varies among brands, and low prices generally yield an inferior product. Look for Hop Sing Lung brand. Oyster sauce should keep indefinitely in the refrigerator.

RICE With few exceptions, rice is central to Asian cuisines and it is a subject worthy of a dissertation. Endless varieties exist in Asia, but they can be divided into two main categories: long grain, which is generally preferred by Chinese, Southeast Asians, and Indians, and short grain, much stickier, and generally preferred by Koreans and Japanese.

Although I keep a short-grain rice, such as Calrose, around to accompany certain dishes, the two that I like best for an all-purpose rice are the fragrant basmati and jasmine. Basmati is a long-grain rice commonly used in Indian cooking. It has a heavenly buttery aroma when cooking and delivers a nutty flavor at the table. Basmati is available in Indian markets in bulk and is also sold in small boxes in Western markets. Jasmine rice is an excellent choice for any recipe in the book where a specific kind of rice is not indicated. This long-grain rice is cultivated in the United States, but some cooks feel that the domestic product does not match the quality of the jasmine rice grown in Thailand. In Asian markets, look for Dragonfly brand, which comes in large sacks. Jasmine rice is also often available in Western supermarkets in boxes of more manageable size.

There are few absolutes when making steamed rice, as the results vary from variety to variety and the ratio of rice to water depends on the amount of rice you're going to cook. When cooking for four people, this is a good rule of thumb: For long-grain rice, rinse 2 cups rice until the water runs clear (this is optional, but I think it improves the rice's texture). To the pot, add $2\frac{1}{4}$ cups water or enough water to come to the first crease of your middle finger (about 1 inch). If you're using a rice cooker—which I highly recommend for easy Asian-style rice—cover and press cook. It will turn off when it's done. Otherwise, proceed to bring the rice and water to a boil, cover, and reduce the heat to low. Cook for 15 to 20 minutes, or until the water is absorbed and the rice is tender. Remove from the heat and let stand, covered, for 5 minutes, then fluff with a fork. You should have about $5\frac{1}{2}$ cups rice.

RICE VINEGAR When a recipe calls for rice vinegar, you're safe using Japanese rice vinegar, which is also the vinegar found most often in supermarkets. Not as harsh as distilled white vinegar, rice vinegar is pale gold. Be sure to purchase an unseasoned vinegar unless the recipe instructs differently. Marukan is a good brand.

RICE WINE, SHAOXING See Shaoxing wine.

SALT, KOSHER Ever since I was introduced to the ease of cooking with kosher salt, I haven't looked back. Kosher salt has a coarser grain than ordinary table salt, so that when you're using your hands rather than a measuring spoon, it is much easier to gauge how much you are adding. Diamond brand is cheap and is sold in its big red box in just about any supermarket. If you have only table salt available, make sure to add less than called for in these recipes and adjust to taste.

SAMBAL OELEK See Chili sauce.

SAUSAGE, CHINESE See Chinese sausage.

SESAME OIL (ROASTED)   A little Asian sesame oil goes a long way, but when used conservatively, adds a great deal of flavor to food. Asian sesame oil is made from roasted sesame seeds and is the color of maple syrup. It has a very low smoke point, making it suitable only as a seasoning, not for frying, unless combined with another oil. (Japanese cooks sometimes season the frying oil for tempura with sesame oil.) The Chinese like to toss a little sesame oil in a stir-fry just before serving to give it a beautiful sheen and nutty fragrance when it arrives at the table. It will go rancid quickly and is best stored in the refrigerator and allowed to come to room temperature before using. Kadoya is a good brand.

SESAME SEEDS   Sesame seeds, both toasted and untoasted, can be purchased in Asian markets. Purists will want to toast their own by putting the seeds in a skillet over medium heat and stirring constantly until the seeds turn a nice nutty brown. Be sure to remove the pan from the heat promptly and pour them onto a plate to cool, or they will continue to darken. Refrigerate sesame seeds to keep them from going rancid. Sesame seeds found in the spice section of mainstream supermarkets are much more expensive than the ones found in Asian markets.

SHAOXING WINE   Shaoxing wine is a Chinese rice wine similar in taste and color to a dry sherry, which can be substituted in a pinch. Do not confuse it with sake, which is Japanese rice wine and very different, and certainly don't try to replace it with rice vinegar. Look for Pagoda brand Shao Hsing Supreme.

SHRIMP, DRIED   See dried shrimp.

SICHUAN PEPPERCORNS   Sichuan peppercorns are not actually peppers, but are instead small berries that come from a bushy shrub. The husks are reddish brown and have a slightly lemony taste. The spice is widely used in Sichuan cuisine for marinades, incorporated with salt to make a popular condiment, and used to season stir-fries and braises. Ground Sichuan pepper is also available, although I find it to be a second-rate alternative. If you are having a hard time finding Sichuan peppercorns, it may be because the USDA bans their import (due to a citrus canker) from time to time.

SOY SAUCE   Soy sauce reigns supreme in China, Korea, and Japan. Made from soybeans that have been mixed with a grain, typically wheat, a generous amount of salt and water, and left to age, soy sauce may be thin (light) or dark (black) and varies in saltiness. I use a thin soy sauce for my recipes. Japanese soy sauces tend to be the most consistent, and a good choice is the familiar Kikkoman. If you want to try an excellent Chinese soy sauce, look for Pearl River Bridge brand.

Soy sauce can be kept indefinitely in the refrigerator. Tamari, a dark, rich Japanese soy sauce made without wheat, has a mellower taste. It should not be substituted for soy sauce in the recipes that call for it in this book.

STAR ANISE Star anise is a beautiful, brown star-shaped spice that comes from a Chinese evergreen tree. The flavor recalls licorice, and the spice is normally used whole. Store in a tightly closed jar in a cool, dark place for up to a year.

TAMARI See Soy sauce.

TAMARIND If you're in the fresh produce section of the market and spot a 4- to 5-inch-long dusky brown pod with an outer shell marked with cracks to reveal a dark brown, sticky interior, you've most likely discovered tamarind. Southeast Asian and Indian recipes make excellent use of this delicious sweet-and-sour fruit and unsuspecting Westerners have delighted in its flavor for years, as it's the main ingredient in Worcestershire sauce. Although tamarind has some of the sourness of lemon or lime, it has a sweetness, too. In Southeast Asian markets, tamarind is sold in bricks or blocks. A piece is cut from the brick, dissolved in hot water (1 part tamarind to 2 parts water), and pushed through a strainer to remove the seeds and fibers before adding to the recipe. In Indian markets, however, you'll find tamarind sold as a concentrate. I've used it in both forms, but for most recipes I prefer the ease that concentrate allows for last-minute cooking. Once the concentrate has been incorporated into a dish, I don't find that the flavor differs dramatically from the brick form.

sources

WEBSITES:

asian-grocery.com
Here is a straightforward, easy-to-navigate site for purchasing Asian ingredients on-line.
You will find few fresh vegetables here, but there is a good selection of canned, bottled, and
dried products.

ethnicgrocer.com
This high-end site claims to be the world's most comprehensive on-line source for ethnic food
ingredients and consumer products from around the globe. They ship within the U.S.

evergreenseeds.com
This site offers more than two hundred varieties of Asian vegetable seeds, which may be ordered
on-line, or contacted by mail at Evergreen Y.H. Enterprises, P.O. Box 17538, Anaheim, CA 92817.

friedas.com
A purveyor of specialty produce, this commercial site has nice descriptions, including nutritional
content, and photos of a variety of Asian vegetables. It points you to stores selling Frieda's produce, or you can order from the site for home delivery in large quantities.

penzeys.com
Penzey's has long been one of my favorite catalogs for spices, and it is now available on-line. A
search for Indian spices brings up forty items.

bibliography

Alford, Jeffrey, and Naomi Duguid. *Seductions of Rice.* New York: Artisan, 1998.

Bladholm, Linda. *The Asian Grocery Store Demystified.* Los Angeles: Renaissance Books, 1999.

Blonder, Ellen, and Annabel Low. *Every Grain of Rice: A Taste of Our Chinese Childhood in America.* New York: Clarkson Potter, 1998.

Cost, Bruce. *Bruce Cost's Asian Ingredients.* New York: William Morrow and Company, Inc., 1988.

Dahlen, Martha. *A Cook's Guide to Chinese Vegetables.* Hong Kong: The Guidebook Company, 1992.

Downer, Lesley. *Japanese Vegetarian Cooking.* New York: Pantheon, 1986.

Durack, Terry. *Noodle.* San Francisco: Soma Books, 1999.

Hom, Ken. *Ken Hom's Asian Ingredients: A Guide with Recipes.* Berkeley: Ten Speed Press, 1996.

Larkom, Joy. *Oriental Vegetables: The Complete Guide for the Gardening Cook.* Tokyo, New York, London: Kodansha International, 1991.

Loha-unchit, Kasma. *It Rains Fishes: Legends, Traditions and the Joys of Thai Cooking.* San Francisco: Pomegranate Artbooks, 1995.

Lo San Ross, Rosa. *Beyond Bok Choy: A Cook's Guide to Asian Vegetables.* New York: Artisan, 1996.

Marks, Copeland, with Manjo Kim. *The Korean Kitchen.* San Francisco: Chronicle Books, 1993.

McDermott, Nancie. *Real Thai.* San Francisco: Chronicle Books, 1992.

Paniz, Neela. *The Bombay Cafe.* Berkeley: Ten Speed Press, 1998.

Pham, Mai. *The Best of Vietnamese and Thai Cooking.* Rocklin, CA: Prima, 1996.

Solomon, Charmaine. *Encyclopedia of Asian Food.* Periplus Editions, 1996.

Tropp, Barbara. *China Moon Cookbook.* New York: Workman, 1992.

———. *The Modern Art of Chinese Cooking.* New York: Hearst, 1982.

Yeo, Chris, and Joyce Jue. *The Cooking of Singapore: Great Dishes from Asia's Culinary Crossroads.* Emeryville, California: Harlow and Ratner, 1993.

Young, Grace. *The Wisdom of the Chinese Kitchen: Classic Family Recipes for Celebration and Healing.* New York: Simon & Schuster Editions, 1999.

index

TABLE OF EQUIVALENTS

The exact equivalents in the following tables have been rounded for convenience.

oven temperature

FAHRENHEIT	CELSIUS	GAS
250	120	1/2
275	140	1
300	150	2
325	160	3
350	180	4
375	190	5
400	200	6
425	220	7
450	230	8
475	240	9
500	260	10

liquid/dry measures

U.S.	METRIC
1/4 teaspoon	1.25 ml
1/2 teaspoon	2.5 ml
1 teaspoon	5 ml
1 tablespoon (3 teaspoons)	15 ml
1 fluid ounce (2 tablespoons)	30 ml
1/4 cup	60 ml
1/3 cup	80 ml
1/2 cup	120 ml
1 cup	240 ml
1 pint (2 cups)	480 ml
1 quart (4 cups, 32 ounces)	960 ml
1 gallon (4 quarts)	3.84 liters
1 ounce (by weight)	28 grams
1 pound	454 grams
2.2 pounds	1 kg